CONFESSIONS
of a SHAMELESS NAME-DROPPER
adventures in the music business

BY MARK CABANISS

BRAVO BOOKS
Brentwood, TN

Copyright © 2013 and 2024 by Melrose House Publishing, LLC

All rights reserved. No part of this book may be reproduced, scanned, stored in a retrieval system or transmitted in any form by any means – electronic, mechanical, photocopy, recording, or otherwise – except for brief quotations for the purpose of review or comment, without prior permission of the publisher, Melrose House Publishing, P.O. Box 3607, Brentwood, Tennessee 37024.

Second edition: July, 2024

Printed in the United States of America

Library of Congress Control Number: 2013919904

Cabaniss, Mark
    Confessions of a Shameless Name-Dropper: Adventures in the Music Business

ISBN 978-0-615-90412-2

Edited by Dimples Kellogg
Cover illustration and design by Tracy Mattocks
Interior design by Jared Collins
Cover design for Revised Edition by Aaron Imbt

DEDICATION

To my nephews: Aaron, Thomas, and Nathan
God gives us talent and challenges us with life.

CONTENTS

Prologue	ix
Overture	xi
Acknowledgments	xiii
1. "Come on Down!" . . . to Hollywood	1
2. "Break Forth" Into the Music Business	11
3. Marian the Librarian	16
4. An Invitation to the Party	24
5. Intermission with Kitty	30
6. Here's Doc! (And Johnny)	34
7. The Norman Conquest	39
8. Prelude to the Press	46
9. Rodgers, Rodgers and Hammerstein	54
10. Hello, Uncle Hal	59
11. Mayberry, Andy, and Me	65
12. The Unsinkable Music Man	73
13. Good-bye, Uncle Hal	85
14. Here on *Gilligan's Island* with *The Brady Bunch*	94
15. Ol' Man Vodka	104
16. The End of Shawnee Press, Inc.	112
17. James Bond Meets James West	119
18. Hi-Ho, Steverino!	126

19. The Game of Word 136
20. Dick Clark's Rockin' Career 144
21. Oz, Jazz, and Judy 148
22. I Kissed a Ghost 154
23. A Man for All Seasons 158
24. New Light Shining 165
25. *Guys and Dolls* and Feuer and Martin 169
26. I Can See Kathie Lee 176
27. *Soli Deo Gloria* 183
Epilogue: The Music of Life 189

PROLOGUE

"A life spent on music is a life beautifully spent."

—Luciano Pavarotti

"The music business is a cruel and shallow money trench, a long plastic hallway where thieves and pimps run free, and good men die like dogs. There's also a negative side."

—Hunter S. Thompson

(I think the truth of the matter probably lies somewhere in between those two statements.)

—Mark Cabaniss

OVERTURE

I'm easily bored.

But people never bore me.

We've seen people throughout history who are capable of the most incredible acts of kindness and love imaginable…and capable of overcoming seemingly impossible odds. We've seen others who are capable of unthinkable and heinous crimes (sometimes with a smile on their faces, even after being caught and convicted). And there are those who are capable of everything in between. But they are all *people* and arrived on planet Earth as *tabula rasa*…blank slates at one time.

Despite the dark side of humanity, I have ultimately never lost faith in the human spirit and the God-given potential for good that lies within everyone.

I'm a "shameless name-dropper" because I like telling the stories of some extraordinary people whom I've had the great fortune to meet and/or work with over the years. The names "dropped" in these pages are people who have inspired and motivated me—and continue to do so – even if they're no longer with us. So I would like to introduce you to these people in hopes they will inspire and motivate you too. Then perhaps you'll shamelessly drop their names as well, because in my opinion, the people and their stories within these pages are worth remembering and sharing.

In addition to inspiring life stories that have the power to transform us, I believe in the transforming power of music, drama, and the arts. I believe that creativity is a gift from God, and when used for good, it has the capacity to change lives in a positive way. Having celebrated my 35th year of work in the music business, I'm offering this updated and revised edition of this book to celebrate the primary One and ones who have inspired me to spend my life in music and other forms of communication that give me the opportunity to fulfill my personal mission statement to hopefully encourage, enlighten, entertain, and/or inspire others.

I consider myself to be very fortunate and blessed to have made my living for so long doing something I love. We spend a lot of time working during our lives. So we might as well enjoy it and help others in the process. And although my professional passions have occasionally come at the expense of some personal pursuits, I don't regret it. Indeed, I am deeply grateful. I agree with Meredith Willson when he said, "My creative endeavors are my children." I'll add that I do hope they'll help take care of me in my old age.

I hope you enjoy these stories. Thank you for taking your time to let me share them with you.

ACKNOWLEDGMENTS

First, I'm obviously indebted to the marvelous and extremely gifted celebrities who are mentioned in this book. I am honored to have met or worked with them, and I appreciate their sharing their time and talents with me. Without them, there would be no names to drop.

My heartfelt thanks go to the editor of the book, Dimples Kellogg. In addition to having a cool name, she is a cool person whose sharp eye and keen observations made this book infinitely better than it would have been without her editorial guidance.

True friends and teachers are a precious commodity, and I am very fortunate to have several. My deepest thanks go to the teachers/mentors who also became friends to me and have helped shape and encourage all my adventures in the music business (and a whole lot more): Mark Blankenship, Gene Ellis, Homer and Marjorie Haworth, C. Robert Jones, Helen Krause, Sharron Lyon, Jean Mauney, Buryl Red, Thomas Rogers, William (Bill) Thomas, Jim Van Hook, and Zig Ziglar

There are other wonderful and dear friends who have helped make my adventures in the music business (and life) a much more pleasant experience. In particular, I can't resist thanking Rosemary Ahmad, Tony Bakker, Lisa Bily, Brenda Crosby Bouser, Bud Christman, Dotty Dickson, Bob and Jackie Dills, Diane Earle, Stan and Janis Gunselman, Angela Heath, Jane Krause Hill, Roxanna Humphries, Ed Kee, Amy Kutz, Aggie Lewis, Dan and Beverly Lunsford, Bruce and Joyce Malony, Ruth Elaine Schram,

ACKNOWLEDGMENTS

Susie Van Hook, Grover and Martha Waller, Frances Welch, Hib and Judy Wiedenkeller, Elizabeth Williams Grayson, and Ginny Thompson Wright.

I add Meredith Willson to this important page, as his life and career have had a tremendous impact on my own. He was truly "the Unsinkable Music Man."

I would also like to thank:

That policeman who didn't give me a speeding ticket; all my family and relatives; Willy Wonka and Mel Stuart; Cleo Laine; Dino Nowak, George and Ira Gershwin; Janet McMahan and Idella; Spike (the noseless wonder); First Baptist Church Shelby; O. V. Hamrick Jr.; Luda, Yuri, and Max; the Hudson Family; Socrates; Cornelius Hackl and Irene Molloy; the gang at Aire Born Recording Studios; Stan Blits and CBS; Curtis Harrington, II; Tommy Thompson; the shark in *Jaws*; Fanny Crosby; the Nalleys and the Whitakers; Kodak; Rex Harrison, Stanley Holloway, and *My Fair Lady*; Mattel; Leroy Anderson; Cheh Bim; that funny woman on the street wearing a kerchief; Susan McCracken and "The Free Phone"; Mary Beth and Mark; Ron Cox and Avenue Bank; Mike McKay and WBTV; Wayne Pressley and Ray Babelay; David Ernst and *Exit*; Mozart; Virginia Waring; Dr. Phil McGraw; football and persistence.

"COME ON DOWN!"...TO HOLLYWOOD

"There's a bad snarl right now on the Hollywood Freeway South," said the traffic announcer on Los Angeles KNX radio.

I should know. I was in the middle of it. And I was on my way to see the iconic TV personality Bob Barker.

I had never met Bob before, and it looked as if I was going to be late! Even though I had allowed almost an hour for a twenty-minute ride, Los Angeles traffic had reared its unsuspecting ugly head at precisely the wrong moment, making what first seemed like a comfortable margin of time to reach Bob now start looking slim.

As the traffic crawled along and I knew my appointment with Bob was scheduled to happen in thirty minutes, I calmed myself, knowing that I could call his publicist if need be to let him know I was running a bit late. But I didn't want to have to do that. I wanted my meeting with this household name to come off without a hitch.

As I drove along, I thought of the famous television show that made Bob Barker a household name, *The Price Is Right*. Actually, when I think about that show, I feel sick.

No, wait. I'll explain.

I can remember when *The New Price Is Right* began on CBS-TV back in

1972. And since those were the days before home video recording devices were invented, the only time I got to see the show was when I was home from school because I was sick, since *Price* aired in the mornings. Of course, I also saw it during holidays and certainly during the summer months. And it made an indelible impression on me, as did its host, Bob Barker.

I think the reason I and millions of others were drawn to the show (aside from Bob) was the sheer fun of the games. I've always enjoyed board games, and *The Price Is Right* seemed to be one mini board game after the next during the show. The show also has plenty of glitz, lights, sound effects, and unpredictable, screaming contestants…let alone well-produced music and lightning-fast camera action and graphics. Plus "the thrill of victory and the agony of defeat." It's a perfect combination that's made it the longest-running game show in television history.

For more than fifty years…*fifty years*…the show has aired daily on CBS. Pretty incredible when you consider how television chews up and spits out new shows by the dozens each year. I also like that the show is very American. It was created by the late game show legend Mark Goodson who, along with long-time business partner Bill Todman, gave birth to shows such as *Beat the Clock*, *Family Feud*, *Match Game*, *Password*, *Tattletales*, *To Tell the Truth*, *I've Got a Secret*, *What's My Line?*, and *Card Sharks*. And although I consider *The Price Is Right* to be very American, it has been re-created in several foreign country versions with great success.

Of all the shows created by Mark Goodson and Bill Todman, *Price* was clearly their greatest success. And at the center of that show was Bob Barker, a broadcaster who, by the end of his career, had racked up fifty astonishing years on television.

So how did I find myself in a traffic jam on the Hollywood Freeway one afternoon on the way to Bob Barker's house? That question can be answered with two words: *Hollywood 360*.

Hollywood 360 is the nationally syndicated radio show that I'd become a part of about a year earlier. I had met Carl Amari, a successful broadcaster and producer based in Chicago (Carl's success story is quite remarkable in and of itself, and if you want to know more about his interesting and impressive career, go to www.hollywood360radio.com and click on the "Your Host" tab at the top of the page). Carl and I seemed to be long-lost brothers due to our mutual interests in broadcasting and classic TV and radio shows. Carl had asked me to do interviews for the show in my spare time as I met various celebrities (during the course of my work) and to be a correspondent for the show.

I said, "Yes," quicker than Jack Benny could foreclose on his mother.

Fast-forward and through a mutual contact, I had met the producer of *The Price Is Right*, Stan Blits. Stan had written a book I'd bought and read a few years earlier about his many years with *The Price Is Right* (titled – of course – *Come On Down!*) so I already knew his name when I connected with him. We were instant friends. He was warm, engaging, and funny... just as you would expect from the producer of a major network game show. As of this writing, Stan has been with *The Price Is Right* for thirty-four years! And he still looks like he's in his thirties. Supports my theory that when we do something we love, it helps keep us young.

"Can you connect me with Bob Barker for an interview for *Hollywood 360*?" I asked Stan.

"Absolutely. Bob has remained very busy, even in retirement. But I'll give you his publicist's contact info, and we'll hope for the best," said Stan.

So with hopes high, I contacted Bob's long-time publicist, Henri Bollinger, and gave him my background information and info about *Hollywood 360*. We seemed to hit it off. He said he would present the idea to Bob, which he did, and I received an e-mail a few days later that Bob had agreed to the interview! And, of all places, it would be conducted in Bob's home in Hollywood! After reading the e-mail, I ran around my house for about a minute celebrating. What fun this would be!

And now, driving to his house, I felt as if I was playing *Beat the Clock*!

As the traffic crawled along on the Hollywood Freeway, I reflected on Bob Barker's amazing career, most of which I'd witnessed through the years and part of which I'd read about as I prepared for my time with him.

Born in Darrington, Washington, Bob enlisted in the United States Navy at the outbreak of World War II (and was a fighter pilot!). After the war, he returned to college to finish his education (working part-time in radio while in school) and graduated *summa cum laude* with a degree in economics.

In 1950, Bob moved to California in order to pursue a career in broadcasting. He was given his own radio show, *The Bob Barker Show*, which ran for the next six years out of Burbank. Bob began his game show career in 1956, hosting *Truth or Consequences*. From there, he hosted various game shows as well as the Miss Universe pageants. Eventually, he hosted *The Price Is Right*, beginning in 1972. When his wife, Dorothy Jo, died, Barker became an advocate for animal rights. Since then, he has been a long-time supporter of animal rights and of animal rights activism, including groups such as the United Activists for Animal Rights and the Sea Shepherd Conservation Society.

Bob's DJ&T Foundation, founded in 1994 and named after his wife, Dorothy Jo, and mother, Tillie, has contributed millions of dollars to fund animal neutering programs, animal rescue, and park facilities all over the United States.

It was on *Truth or Consequences* that a salute became his trademark sign-off; he ended each episode with "Bob Barker saying good-bye, everybody, and hoping all your consequences are happy ones!"

In 1987, Barker did what other emcees almost never did: renounced hair dye and allowed his hair to turn gray. Fellow hosts Monty Hall, Alex Trebek, and Richard Dawson would do the same in the late 1980s.

Bob took over the role of executive producer for *The Price Is Right* in 1988, following the death of the original executive producer, Frank Wayne. In this capacity, Barker created several pricing games, instituted a prohibition on foreign cars and animal-based products, and launched a prime-time series of specials known as *The Price Is Right $1,000,000 Spectacular*.

Bob holds the record of being the oldest man ever to host a regularly scheduled television game show and the oldest man ever to host a weekday television program since the inception of American network television. Barker also hosted or appeared on a five-day-a-week television program longer than anyone else in the history of television.

Bob has won a total of nineteen Emmy Awards. Fourteen were for Outstanding Game Show Host, more than any other performer. He has also won four for Executive Producer of *The Price Is Right* and received the Lifetime Achievement Award for Daytime Television in 1999. On April 9, 1998, on the occasion of the ceremonial five thousandth episode of *The Price Is Right*, CBS named the sound stage (Studio 33, where the show has been produced since 1972) "The Bob Barker Studio." In 2004, Bob was inducted into the Academy of Television Arts & Sciences Hall of Fame.

In 2007, Bob was inducted into the Hall of Famous Missourians, and a bronze bust depicting him is on permanent display in the rotunda of the Missouri State Capitol. Also in 2007, *Time* named Barker the greatest game show host of all time, claiming that he "never lost his utterly natural charm or self-effacing people skills." That same year, Bob retired from hosting *The Price Is Right* after celebrating his fifty-year career on television. On April 14, 2008, Bob was inducted to the National Association of Broadcasters' Broadcasting Hall of Fame.

And that is the man I was about to be late to see!

Fortunately, after nonstop prayer (and some aggressive driving), the traffic cleared up and I made it to Bob's house…with five minutes to spare! I now had the luxury of re-reviewing my prepared questions. I parked on the street and collected my thoughts. Then, precisely one minute before the appointed interview time, I drove into his driveway. Bob, along with Henri, came out of the house to greet me. Shaking his hand, I introduced myself, and Bob smiled that trademark smile and invited me in.

Bob's house is located in Hollywood not far off one of the main streets. Knowing where CBS Television City is located (where *Price* has taped all these years), I figured Bob had about a fifteen-minute drive each day when he was doing the show. Not bad. His house is a beautiful Spanish-style adobe stucco. He told me his late wife loved the house so much that she hoped it wouldn't be torn down and converted into something after she and he were gone (knowing that she was terminally ill). So Bob did some research and found out that it qualified to be listed in the cultural register of California landmarks. So it is safe thanks to his efforts.

The three of us sat in his study and began our visit. Even now, he looked much younger than his eighty-something years. I could tell immediately he still had energy, enthusiasm, and ebullience for life. Retirement had been good to Bob, I thought.

"Let's talk about *Truth or Consequences* first, Bob. How did that show happen for you?"

"Well, [legendary TV host and producer] Ralph Edwards started the show years and years ago in radio, before television. In fact, it was the most popular radio show in the United States in 1941. I was in Los Angeles doing local radio shows when Ralph got a commitment from the new NBC Television to air *Truth or Consequences* five days a week. He didn't want to host the show for TV, so he auditioned hosts in New York and LA.

"Ralph just happened to turn on my radio show, and he liked the way I worked. So he called me in and I went through a series of auditions, and on December 21st, 1956, at five minutes past noon, he called me and said I was the man. I got the job. It was my first national show. And on every December 21st after that, Ralph and I had lunch together, and at five minutes after noon, we had a toast to our long, enduring friendship. And we did that for the rest of his life."

After hosting *Truth or Consequences* for nineteen years, certainly Bob had some favorite memories. Bob immediately started chuckling.

"Yes, one of my favorite stunts involved a cute boy, who seemed to be about eight or nine. We had invited a local Little League team to the show and after doing the audience warm-up, I started walking around the audience to select contestants as I always did for each show. Of course, I knew about the Little League team and spotted this cute kid among them, and after talking to him for a bit, I knew he would be the perfect ball player to feature from the team.

"During the show, I brought this kid up onstage and told him he was going to be at bat, and that he could hit the ball as hard as he wanted into a curtain off stage. The kid was ready to go and couldn't wait to knock that ball out of the studio.

"Unbeknownst to this kid and the audience, we'd also invited two young girls who were professional softball players. They looked like regular audience members, and I pretended to randomly select them to come onstage and serve as the pitcher and catcher.

"Well, the boy batter thought he had it made when I selected these two girls. Now he was chomping at the bit to hit that ball even harder.

"So the girl pitcher throws the first pitch and *WHAM*…it went so fast past that kid you could hardly see it. *BAM* it went into the other girl's catcher's mitt. It happened so fast the boy at bat didn't know what hit him. He was stunned. He said, 'That's an artificial ball!'

"So I grabbed the ball and showed it to him and said, 'There's nothing wrong with this ball. Take a look.'

"So then comes pitch number two from this girl softball hustler. Again… *WHAM* and *BAM*! The boy was even more stunned and frustrated. He said, 'That girl has an artificial arm!'"

Bob was laughing so hard he could hardly continue.

"By now, the audience was screaming with laughter. And the little boy's eyes were as big as saucers. Of course, I let him in on the joke, and he laughed as well. But I think he was mostly relieved that the reason he couldn't hit the ball from this supposedly random audience pitcher was because it was a set-up. His honor was restored in front of millions of viewers and especially his teammates who were in the audience."

Next, we shifted to *The Price Is Right*.

"*The Price Is Right* had been a very successful show on radio and early television, too, with Bill Cullen. They would basically bring items to a table and have contestants guess prices. The only thing on the earlier version that resembled the show I did was Contestants' Row…when they bid from the floor to get up on stage.

"But [*Price Is Right* creator and producer] Mark Goodson, in all his wisdom, realized that the original version was really too slow for television and there wasn't enough action. So he came up with the idea of these pricing games. When he first called me in to discuss hosting, he told me he only had five games so far.

"After we discussed it for a bit, I said to him, 'Mark, I think this will work…I think you may have something here'—which was the understatement of all time! He agreed and said, 'I think we'll have a good run,' but he – nor I – never imagined it would last as long as it has."

Was there a favorite game Bob had during all those years?

"Clearly 'Plinko' is the audience's favorite game. I liked 'Plinko' too. But what I really liked were the games where I could build excitement and have fun with the contestant. For example, there was a game where the contestant could win not one or two but three cars! I would get the contestant onstage and say, 'You've got a chance to win this!' and the doors would fly open, and there was a new car. And then I would say, 'But you could also win *this*!' Again, the doors would fly open, and there was another new car. By now the audience was screaming and the contestant absolutely euphoric. But then, I would say, 'But that's not all! You could also win *this*!' A third set of doors would open, and there was a third car! By now, the audience was bouncing off the walls and the contestant was out of their mind. I really enjoyed those moments when I could really get things going."

Does Bob ever watch the show these days?

"Occasionally I watch just to see what's going on, and I must tell you, when they hired Drew Carey to host I had never met him. So when I did meet him before he started hosting, while I was shaking his hand – before we had even finished shaking hands – he said, 'Bob, I'm going to continue to do your spay/neuter plug at the end for as long as I host the show.' I really appreciate that…Drew is my man."

What question might I ask that he hadn't been asked before after countless interviews?

"After doing *The Price Is Right* for all those years, Bob, take us back to that moment at the beginning of the show when the iconic theme is playing, the audience is on their feet screaming and applauding as Johnny Olson shouts, 'Come on down!' and then says your name. The doors open, and you step out into that controlled chaos. What must that have felt like?"

"I never ceased enjoying it. I have been blessed because I started doing audience participation shows way back in Springfield, Missouri, and from then on never had a day in my entire career when I got up and said, 'Oh, I don't want to go to work today.' I loved it. And I think the shows I did were successful in part because I enjoyed it so much, and the audience enjoyed it along with me. I frequently say had it not been for television, I would have had to work for a living."

As our time was beginning to come to a close, I felt compelled to tell Bob exactly how I felt about his career and approach to his craft.

"Bob, to me, you are and will always be the Gold Standard of broadcasters. And when I think of you the word *class* comes to mind. You have always respected the relationship between host and audience, and never abused it. I could always tell you never took for granted the privilege of entering millions of homes on a daily basis for fifty years. You built a relationship of trust with your audience for all those years, and that's one of many reasons we all enjoyed inviting you back, year after year…decade after decade."

He smiled a broad smile and offered his heartfelt thanks. "I owe it all to the audience. Without them, no one would have ever heard of Bob Barker," he said.

I then told Bob that in the presence of a broadcasting icon, I couldn't close the interview with him sitting there; only he could. He smiled and launched into it without missing a beat: "Well, it's a profound thought: Help control the pet population. Have your pet spayed or neutered!"

As I was leaving his home, I insisted that I make a donation to Bob's DJ&T Foundation (even though he said it certainly wasn't expected). I told him it would make me happy to donate, and so he agreed. Shortly after I'd sent my small gift to the foundation, I received a handwritten note from Bob on his personally engraved stationery thanking me for my donation and wishing me his best.

Bob Barker is a class act, even when millions aren't listening or watching.

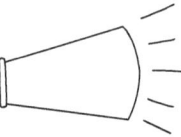

WAIT, WAIT… THERE'S MORE!

The day before I met with Bob, my friend Stan Blits who produces *The Price Is Right* got me a VIP pass to see the show being taped…which included entering the famed CBS Television City though the artist's entrance and getting a parking space with my name on it the day of the show. The show taping itself was everything you would imagine…high energy and pure fun. After the taping, he took me on a backstage tour of Studio 33 (now named The Bob Barker Studio) and let me spin the iconic wheel. Hilarious and pure pop culture fun!

"BREAK FORTH" INTO THE MUSIC BUSINESS

It took that proverbial snowball hurtling through hell to get me into the music business. And it all started with a phone call when I was twenty-three years old.

One summer afternoon, while I was in my hometown of Shelby for semester break from graduate school at the University of Tennessee, I got a phone call from Ludy Wilkie. Yes, his name is Ludy (pronounced *LOO-dee*). I have no idea where that name came from. Sounds like an early model car.

"Yes, I drive a Ludy with Naugahyde interior," I could hear someone say. Ludy is about as eccentric as his name (and as durable as Naugahyde), but a delightful and talented guy and I'd always enjoyed my contacts with him, though limited.

"I'm writing a reader's theatre adaptation of the Gospel of Luke," said Ludy. "I know you've done some composing" (he'd heard some of my music before). He continued, "I would like for you to write the music for the texts I've selected to be included in the piece."

I guess you could say this was my first commissioned work—but with no money attached, at least not yet. I had never had anyone call and ask *me* to write music or lyrics.

I said, "Yes," faster than you can say Lennon and McCartney.

The next day, we met and he gave me six texts (all neatly typed on his IBM Selectric Typewriter…remember?) to set to music. I jumped right in. The one text that leapt off the page to me was actually not from the Gospel of Luke but from Isaiah. It started out, "Burst into songs of joy, you ruins of Jerusalem…"

One of the translations of the text I found started out "Break forth into joy…" (instead of "Burst into songs"), and that sounded more poetic to me and certainly would sing easier than "burst into…" I made other minor changes to the text as well to make it more poetic, while keeping the essence intact. After I'd written the first draft, I called my friend Dotty Dickson.

Dotty lived in the same neighborhood in which I'd been reared, and although I had known her as "Mrs. Dickson" while growing up, due to my involvement in the local community theatre during high school and college, she had become Dotty to me as a dear friend and mentor. She was (and is) very encouraging to me in my writing and career and taught me music theory and composition in high school. Not only did she nurture my interest in music, composing, and theatre, when I went to college and majored in music, her lessons helped make freshman music theory a breeze.

So I got in the car and hurried up the street to see Dotty with my new creation in hand.

After carefully listening to the piece, Dotty simply and wisely said, "It needs a bridge." (For the uninformed, a musical bridge is a contrasting section between other musical sections in a piece that bridges those sections together.) As usual, Dotty was right. I went back home immediately and wrote a bridge. It seemed right then.

In the next few weeks, I had completed all the choral and piano arranging for *Break Forth Into Joy*, and back at grad school that fall, I completed the other five pieces for Ludy's work.

Of the six total pieces I'd written for the work, I felt strongest about *Break Forth Into Joy* and hoped this could be the piece that would get me my first published composition. So I packed the piece up and started sending it out to publishers as an unsolicited manuscript.

Having been in the music business for over thirty-five years now and reviewing hundreds – if not thousands – of unsolicited manuscripts in my role at various music publishers, I see what an incredible long shot (truly a "snowball's chance") that my little piece would be picked up by a major publisher. But very naïvely I sent it out to a few leading publishers with high hopes, along with a demo cassette (yes, *cassette*…remember?).

The rejection letters came back sometimes swiftly, sometimes not. But come they did. So I shelved the piece (literally, in my bedroom closet), and there it sat for about a year collecting the proverbial dust. I was disappointed and disheartened. I believed in that piece, but apparently no one else did.

Fast-forward now to 1985. I had been out of grad school for a year and had taken my first job in Owensboro, Kentucky, teaching at Kentucky Wesleyan College. I was at Wednesday night choir rehearsal, and the director passed out a choral piece published by a company I'd never heard of before: Brentwood Music. It was located in Brentwood, Tennessee, which I'd also never heard of before. I would soon learn that Brentwood is a suburb of Nashville. I wondered whether this publisher might be interested in taking a look at *Break Forth Into Joy*. I had nothing to lose, and one of my many maxims in life is nothing ventured; nothing gained. So I dusted the piece off and sent it in (though with little hope of the piece being published).

About a month passed and I'd all but forgotten about sending the piece out or at least given up any major hopes that it would be published once and for all. Then when I was returning to my office at the college from lunch one fall day, I saw a note on my door. It was written by a student who had taken a phone call for me in my absence. It simply read: "Call Sarah Griffith. Brentwood Music."

There was also a phone number scribbled on the note. I was very excited, yet cautious. My mind was racing. Certainly, this person and Brentwood Music wouldn't be calling to give me a personal rejection of the piece on the phone. They must be interested in publishing it! I didn't have long to ponder these things because in a matter of seconds after reading the message, I was calling Sarah Griffith at Brentwood Music.

I got Ms. Griffith on the phone, and she was very complimentary about the piece and said of all the "boxes full of unsolicited manuscripts" she'd reviewed for their upcoming publishing cycle, this one jumped out at her.

"Have you placed it elsewhere yet?" Sarah asked. "No. Not yet" was my quick reply (little did she know!). She said she'd shared the piece and demo recording with Jim Van Hook, president and founder of Brentwood Music, and he liked it too. "We would like to publish your piece for a spring 1986 release date."

Of course, I was elated. After I hung up, I broke forth into joy right there in my office. I eventually became friends with Sarah Griffith, who later became Sarah Huffman. I hired her more than twenty years later to be my senior editorial director at Word Music, let alone utilizing her as a vocal contractor/studio singer—which she did in those days—and editor for dozens and dozens of pieces I subsequently published.

I dedicated *Break Forth Into Joy* to my beloved high school choral director, Helen Cole Krause. When I surprised and presented Helen with the handwritten manuscript and published piece along with it (her name at the top of the music), she was speechless. Here was a woman who, with great humor, inspiration, dedication, talent, discipline, and love, had inspired thousands of music students, especially me, over her long and successful teaching career. Dedicating the piece to her was the nicest thing about the entire experience of having my first-ever published composition.

The piece went on to be one of Brentwood Music's biggest sellers that year. I am eternally grateful to Jim Van Hook and Sarah Griffith Huffman for taking a chance on an unknown composer and his music. Thanks to them, according to my royalty statements, *Break Forth Into Joy* has been performed to date by more than 100,000 singers since its publication and heard by around a million people (and, as of this writing, is still in print).

Not bad for the little snowball that could.

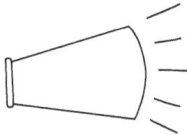

WAIT, WAIT... THERE'S MORE!

Speaking of Helen Krause, I would later found and fund an endowed music scholarship in Helen's name to be used at my alma mater, Mars Hill University. We announced the scholarship publicly with a dinner in Shelby, featuring entertainment from my best and most talented friends from high school. I was honored that Dan Lunsford (now former) president of Mars Hill University, along with (now former) VP Bud Christman and other Mars Hill brass, attended and spoke. We closed the evening with an alumni chorus singing "A Parting Blessing" (written by J. Jerome "Jim" Williams), which has become a modern choral classic (published by Shawnee Press). Helen conducted the song, and Jim, though just returning from a long trip to Europe that afternoon and not even unpacked yet, made a special effort to attend the event in Helen's honor, whom he adores. Being the president of Shawnee Press at the time with Helen conducting that particular piece with my best high school friends singing, plus many family and other local friends and former teachers looking on, made it one of those evenings I wanted to bronze and keep forever. Unforgettable!

MARIAN THE LIBRARIAN

It was a warm spring afternoon in Los Angeles. I was there on a business trip and had just wrapped up a meeting. Fighting the late afternoon rush-hour traffic, I didn't want to be late because I was on my way to meet with one of my heroes…Shirley Jones.

Star of films such as *Oklahoma!, Carousel, Elmer Gantry, The Music Man*, and many more, Shirley Jones had also starred as the mom on TV's *The Partridge Family* in the 1970s. I glanced at my watch and knew I had to push hard to get there on time. I had only fifteen minutes before I was to be on her doorstep, and as I maneuvered through the traffic, I started thinking about some of my favorite Shirley moments on film and TV. *The Partridge Family* came up first since that was how I first "met" her.

For the uninitiated, *The Partridge Family* was a successful TV show back in the 1970s on ABC-TV. Based on the real-life Rhode Island family band The Cowsills, it starred Shirley as a single mother raising five children, who – along with her – were a traveling pop band. Her real-life stepson, David Cassidy, was also in the show – playing one of her sons. To me as a kid, the idea that a family could make a living by making music was fascinating and cool. Not only was the show typical entertaining sitcom fare, it also had some nice pop tunes integrated into the show each week. Other than the 1960s show *The Monkees*, I can't think of another program that wove in pop tunes on a weekly basis (and today's generation thinks *Glee* started it). Screen Gems was the studio that produced *The Monkees*, and it was looking for another follow-up hit to that series when a producer had the idea for this new show. *The Partridge Family* was also a bit groundbreaking in its own way because Shirley portrayed one of the first single working moms on television.

From 1970 to 1974 during the run of *The Partridge Family*, the fictional singing group racked up six gold albums and seven *Billboard* Top 40 hits (including several Top 10 hits). Not bad for a "family" that couldn't sing! Well, Shirley and David sang, and of course, David Cassidy became the real magic in the musical success of the show. There's no question the popularity of the series started my early interest in the music business (and probably a lot of other ten-year-old kids at the time).

With that as the backdrop, I drove up to the home of Shirley Jones and her husband, Marty Ingels. It was situated covertly off the road and required a security code to enter, which her agent had given to me in advance. I entered the code and the gate opened. Fortunately, I was right on time.

So how did I get from Nashville to Shirley Jones's front door?

About a year before this adventure, the Iowa Choral Directors Association invited me to be one of the featured clinicians at their annual convention (full details on that experience later). The convention was to be held in Mason City that year – Meredith Willson's famous hometown (which he called "River City" in his hit musical, *The Music Man*). I was thrilled at the prospect of going to Mason City because of its connection with Meredith and *The Music Man*. My association with the Iowa Choral Directors eventually connected me with Carl Miller, the president of The Music Man Square – a multimillion-dollar museum and foundation in Mason City dedicated to preserving Meredith Willson's legacy and furthering music education.

After I spent a few days in Mason City with Carl, he asked me to serve on the Board of Advisors for The Music Man Square. I was honored and delighted to do so. Carl (and Meredith's widow, Rosemary) had approached Shirley about supporting The Music Man Square as well, and being the gracious person she is, Shirley was supportive of their efforts.

"You need to meet Shirley," Carl said. "I think the two of you together could dream up some great ideas for The Music Man Square." He didn't have to suggest that again. I was more than happy to meet with Shirley and support the cause in which we both believed.

Shirley opened the door and greeted me with a warm smile (looking at least twenty years younger than she has a right to...all natural, by the way, I'm told by those in the know). She invited me into her living room, and her husband, Marty, soon came into the room to greet me as well (he still sounds like he left Brooklyn yesterday). A certain manic energy surrounded him, even off-camera. After a brief visit, Marty excused himself so that Shirley and I could begin our chat.

Within a few minutes the phone rang. Shirley politely excused herself to answer it, and while she was out, I walked around her living room enjoying her memorabilia...everything from family pictures to her Academy Award. A minute later, as she walked back into the room, I happened to be standing next to her grand piano. I couldn't resist, so I started playing the song "Goodnight, My Someone" from *The Music Man*. She paused, looked at me, smiled, and said simply, "Isn't that a lovely song?" Here was the actress who sang that song as Marian the Librarian in *The Music Man* film, which has been seen by millions over the years, and yet she didn't seem to be impressed by herself one bit.

After the usual pleasantries, I asked her the question I'm sure she's gotten a thousand times before: Just how did you get your start in show business?

"In New York City, my voice teacher convinced me to audition for a Broadway agent, Gus Schirmer," she said. Schirmer was pleased to put her under contract, and with her parents' approval, she settled in New York City and gave herself one year to become a Broadway performer. She only had $100 in her pocket. If she did not succeed, she would move back to her hometown of Smithton, Pennsylvania, and study to be a veterinarian.

Her first audition was for an open biweekly casting call held by John Fearnley, casting director for Rodgers and Hammerstein and their various musicals. At the time, Jones had never heard of Rodgers and Hammerstein. Ken Welch (who, along with his wife, Mitzi, was later a writer for *The Carol Burnett Show*) encouraged Shirley to audition.

"Kenny Welch was a good friend. I was on my way to college, and he said I should audition. He said it would be fun and good experience for me. So I did." The role she was to audition for was a chorus replacement part in the long-running *South Pacific*.

Fearnley was so impressed with Shirley's audition that he ran across the street to fetch Richard Rodgers, who was rehearsing with an orchestra for an upcoming musical. Rodgers loved what he heard and saw, then called Oscar Hammerstein at home. Soon, Hammerstein was sitting in the theatre listening to young Shirley sing. He then asked an odd question for someone who was auditioning for a role in *South Pacific*.

"Do you know the score for *Oklahoma!*?"

"I know the music but not the words," she replied.

"We'll get you a score," said Hammerstein. The next day, Shirley found herself in front of a full orchestra in a Broadway theatre singing several songs from *Oklahoma!*, including the signature song "People Will Say We're in Love."

"My knees were shaking as I sang for them," she told me. "But somehow, I got through it."

The great Rodgers and Hammerstein saw enormous potential in Shirley, and she got the part. But they didn't take special interest in her simply as a replacement chorus role. Unbeknownst to Shirley, they were looking for the lead female for the upcoming film version of their earlier landmark musical *Oklahoma!*, which was scheduled to begin shooting the following year. After hearing Shirley and spending time with her, they knew they'd found their Laurey. (She said the film was actually shot in Arizona, not Oklahoma.)

Rodgers and Hammerstein were so impressed with Shirley, she became the first and only singer to be put under personal contract with the songwriters.

"Dick Rodgers was my guru, my teacher," she said. "I learned an enormous amount from both Dick and Oscar." I asked her if it was true that Dick Rodgers's legendary meticulousness as a composer who not only wanted his music to be performed correctly, but consistently during the run of a show was true.

"Every week, Dick would come to the theatre, and there would be a piano on stage and he would run the entire show playing the piano with the whole cast to make sure they were singing it correctly. It really kept things fresh and tight during the often long runs of their shows."

Other film musicals quickly followed for Shirley, including *Carousel*, *April Love* (1957), and *The Music Man*, in which she was often typecast as a wholesome, kind character. However, she won a 1960 Academy Award for her performance in *Elmer Gantry* portraying a woman corrupted by the title character played by Burt Lancaster. Her character becomes a prostitute who encounters her seducer years later and takes her revenge.

We talked about *The Partridge Family* next. She said her agent warned her about doing the show when she was approached by the producers to star in the series.

"My agent said, 'Are you crazy? Don't even think about doing a TV series. It will kill your movie career.'" But Shirley had been filming movies all over the world, and with young children at home, she wanted to be able to be close to help raise her family.

"I knew doing a TV series would help keep me at home, since it would be filmed completely here in Los Angeles," she explained. "The show did end up hurting my movie career, but it was worth it."

As for her stepson, David Cassidy, who costarred in the show and became the biggest teen idol since Elvis Presley: "The producers of the show had no idea what they had when they cast David. They knew he could act and play the guitar but were completely unaware of his incredible singing voice."

The producers soon figured out they had a gold mine on their hands with Cassidy. And he became the jet fuel that catapulted the series and its associated merchandise – records, magazines, lunch boxes, T-shirts, etc. – into the stratosphere. The show lasted for four seasons and started running out of gas only when two factors played into its ultimate demise.

"The network moved us from our Friday night slot to Saturday night opposite *All in the Family*. Of course, that show was breaking new ground and was unstoppable. Any show would have failed against it."

The other major factor for *The Partridge Family* losing steam was David Cassidy's growing indifference toward the show by its fourth season.

"David was touring all over the world by then and wanting to do more rock music, not the type of music he was performing on the show each week. When he announced he was leaving the show, we knew the show probably couldn't last without him." So after four and a half seasons, *The Partridge Family* left the air. Shirley stayed in regular contact with her stepson David Cassidy until he passed away. And she stays in touch with the other cast members from the show. All except Susan Dey.

"Susan is a lovely person, but I'm disappointed she decided to distance herself from the show. It was her first big break in show business, and I would think she would be proud of it – and grateful. But we all make our choices."

I shifted gears to talk about my favorite musical, *The Music Man*.

Here was a full-fledged musical at a time when Broadway musicals being transferred to film was starting to become a dying art. *The Music Man* is one of the last big-budget Hollywood film versions of successful Broadway musicals from the Golden Age of Broadway.

Shirley spoke of her fondness for the entire experience: "I was thrilled to get the part in the film. I had seen the show on Broadway but after Robert Preston had left it and Burt Parks was playing the lead."

She spoke of the immortal Robert Preston, as Harold Hill, next: "Bob was wonderful. He'd performed the role over a thousand times on Broadway, but he never once said to me or anyone else on the set, 'This is the way we always did it on Broadway.' He approached the film as if he was doing the show for the first time."

I told her I'd heard choreographer Onna White, who had choreographed the original Broadway production and also choreographed the film, was quite a fun character.

"Oh yes! Onna was something else and delightful in her own way. I was a bit nervous about the dancing in the film – especially the 'Shipoopi' number—and said that to Onna. She told me, 'Honey, by the time you finish this film, you'll be a dancer.' And she never let me doubt it otherwise."

Another amazing thing about the filming of *The Music Man* was that a few weeks into the shoot, Shirley discovered she was pregnant, the most dreaded film production word in the English language. Unsure as to how to handle it, she asked for a lunch meeting with the film's director, Morton DaCosta. And while Morton (nicknamed "Tec" – pronounced "Teak") shared Shirley's joy about her news, he knew others in the production company would become nervous that the film wouldn't be completed now that Shirley was with child. "Nobody must know…nobody," warned Tec. "We'll wrap you in sashes and bows as you show more and more," he added. But, Shirley said, Robert Preston eventually found out about the pregnancy accidentally.

"It was finale day and we were shooting the magical footbridge scene where Professor Harold Hill [Preston] and Marian the Librarian finally embrace and kiss and sing their way into a glorious Happy Ever After."

She continued, "At this point, I was standing on the footbridge, looking at Harold Hill and ready to sing 'Till There Was You.'

"It's the third take…the music begins, Preston reaches out for me and pulls me close…very close…begins to speak…and sing…when suddenly… *BOOM*…Bob LEAPS back a giant three-foot leap…piercing the humongous soundstage with his great, round baritone: 'What the hell was that???'"

Shirley added, "The music stopped. Nobody moved, nobody spoke, everybody waiting for the earth to open somewhere and save the day for all of us."

Finally, Meredith Willson spoke from the back of the giant soundstage, breaking the silence, his words resonating as if they were spoken from the Grand Canyon: "That, Mister Preston, was Patrick William Cassidy."

Shirley said the laughter started slowly, then grew to envelop everybody.

"I guess it was very much in keeping with the joy on *The Music Man* set that reflected Meredith Willson's labor of love to the very last shot on the very last day."

Fast-forward around twenty-two years later, when the all-grown-up Patrick Cassidy was attending a Broadway show that starred Robert Preston. Of course, Patrick had heard all his life the story of him startling Preston from his mother's stomach once upon a time. Cassidy couldn't wait to meet Preston at last, so he went backstage after the show. After being ushered into Preston's dressing room, he said, "Mr. Preston, I'm Patrick Cassidy."

Without missing a beat, Preston responded, "I know. We've already met."

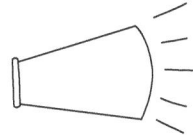

WAIT, WAIT... THERE'S MORE!

To learn much more about Shirley Jones, read her fascinating and revealing book *Shirley Jones: A Memoir*.

AN INVITATION TO THE PARTY

"*Break Forth Into Joy* is selling well. You should send us some more pieces."

I suddenly heard Handel's "Hallelujah Chorus" in my head.

The words were from Ed Kee, who was then creative director at Brentwood Music…three months after my little "snowball's chance" piece had been released.

"…is selling well." Those are three beautiful words in the music biz, especially to a novice composer as I was in those days. I love to hear them now too!

Ed spoke those words to me at an event in Owensboro, Kentucky (where I was still living then). He was there to present Brentwood Music's newest pieces to a large gathering of church choral directors and had asked me to present my piece to the group. Of course, this was the proverbial music to my ears. Getting my first piece of music into print had whetted my appetite for more, and I was eager to provide him with additional works.

I told Ed I had a business trip to Nashville in about a month, and perhaps we could get together for lunch and I could bring him some more pieces. He said we should definitely get together. We did so, and that eventually led to me laying my cards on the table a few lunches later.

"I would love to work at Brentwood Music," I said.

"Mark, that may happen someday," he replied. "I think you would fit in nicely. But at this point, we don't have any openings. Just sit tight. We're growing fast, and that will create some opportunities someday."

Someday? I was eager to get started *right then*. Besides, although I basically liked what I was doing, I was hemorrhaging to get into the music business. But I knew I needed to be patient, and I would also try and knock on other doors as well, which I did.

Eventually Ed said, "You need to meet Jim." I didn't know who that was, but I would soon find out. "Jim" was none other than Jim Van Hook, the founder and president of Brentwood Music. Brentwood was still a relatively small company in those days, but as Ed had indicated, it was growing at a rapid rate. Jim had experienced a very successful career in the music business before founding Brentwood Music. He had been a college professor at the tender age of twenty-three, then became minister of music at the largest Nazarene church in the United States (in Oklahoma) and built a huge music program at that church. This effort got him noticed by several major evangelical sacred publishers in Nashville. Along the way, he'd also dabbled in various music-related entrepreneurial activities. All this led to his being named as the senior vice president of The Benson Company in Nashville, the oldest Christian record and publishing company (in those days) in the world.

Although Jim eventually became the heir apparent at Benson, then President Bob Benson's death led to an unexpected change in executive management. Suddenly, Jim was no longer the heir apparent. He knew he needed to find other career opportunities. So to move his career to the next level, Jim founded Brentwood Music in 1981. He lived in the Nashville "bedroom community" of Brentwood, and that's how the company got its name.

An entire book could be written about the challenges, triumphs, and ultimate amazing success of Jim Van Hook and Brentwood Music. But for our purposes here, I will tell you that it was a series of best-selling concept records that really put Brentwood Music on the map and secured its financial footing. A "concept record" isn't artist-related but is driven by a concept. "Beside Still Waters" (lush sacred music using the panpipes with full orchestra) and "Smoky Mountain Hymns" (gospel hymns played on hand-crafted instruments like the fiddle and mandolin) were smash hits for Brentwood, selling millions of copies. Some of the big Christian record labels in Nashville snickered at first about some of Brentwood's releases, but Jim was laughing all the way to the bank for years and years, while quietly building what became the most profitable Christian music record label in the industry in those days.

Jim and I hit it off immediately. We had a lot in common. We were both trumpet players and had directed choirs over the years. We had both taught college at a young age. Also, his parents had retired in my hometown, and although I had never met them before, we found out we had mutual friends through them. If that weren't enough, we somewhat resembled each other and wore the same size clothing!

Jim was warm, very bright, very successful, down to earth, and a hard worker. And an incredible businessman. Not to mention a fine musician. By the time I met him, he'd already had a very successful career. I knew I wanted to work for him.

What followed in the years to come – yes, three years to be exact before he hired me – was the routine of me driving to Nashville from Owensboro, having lunch with Jim to see what was happening at Brentwood Music (so that I could learn specifically about his current challenges), and then writing him a thank-you letter after our lunch (of course, this was before the days of e-mail) to offer solutions to his problems, which I could implement for his company. I then faithfully checked my post office box daily at the college, hoping every single day I would receive a response from Jim Van Hook. And he did, indeed, always write cordial and encouraging responses to my letters. It was always a very special day when I saw that light blue envelope in my post office box with the Brentwood Music logo on it. I hoped it was my invitation to the music business "party." And compared to what eventually happened to the music business financial model, indeed it was a party in those days.

So if the music business was a party in the 1980s, my party invitation arrived on Tuesday, January 24, 1989. That was the day that Jim Van Hook offered me a job at Brentwood Music.

We were having lunch at a restaurant in Franklin, Tennessee, not far from where Brentwood Music was located. There had been many lunches with Jim in prior years, and I often thought he might "pop the question." But it had never happened. But today was to be the day. About halfway through lunch, Jim leaned in and spoke. He had a smile on his face.

"I've got a job for you at Brentwood Music," he said. "Would you like to join us?"

It was as if Jim had stamped my passport, and now I could go anywhere.

I said, "Yes," faster than a Baptist preacher passes the offering plate.

My first day at Brentwood Music was about six months later, on July 5. I reported to Jim, and he patiently taught me worlds about the music business. The six years that followed while I was at Brentwood are among the happiest in my professional life. It was a series of "firsts": product development, sales, marketing, producing, publishing, cover designs, and more. It was the best education in the music business I could have ever received—all in a familial environment.

Brentwood Music truly felt like a family in those days, and everyone who was there at that time still remembers it that way. I was happy and honored to be a part of the family. (I served as the emcee at Brentwood Music's 20th anniversary party in 2001, and it was a very special evening as more than a hundred former employees, spouses, and friends of Brentwood Music celebrated "the good old days" of the company.)

Six months into my tenure, Jim told me he was in final talks to acquire the print music rights for the John W. Peterson catalog. Peterson was a legendary composer of church music in his day, and although his heyday was over, his print music still sold steadily and had a following. Jim asked if I would be interested in helming this new division of Brentwood Music.

Jim had originally hired me to explore direct marketing for Brentwood Music, but I knew this was my chance to do precisely what I had always wanted to do in the music business: produce, publish, and work with writers. I jumped at the chance.

We named the new division Designer Music Group, and I told Jim we should target it to the mainline/traditional church since Brentwood Music was already reaching the evangelical church. He agreed, and Designer Music Group was off and running in January 1990. In six months, I had moved from being a college professor to a music publisher-producer.

And I loved it. Not only did I produce and publish print music releases, but also numerous concept records…from string quartet recordings to children's recordings and videos. In one year, Designer Music Group went from zero in sales to a more than $1 million division.

Six years later, things had shifted slightly at Brentwood Music, and I was head of the Brentwood Music print division in addition to my duties as head of Designer Music. Although I was happy in my work there, I was beginning to get a little restless. I had aspirations of becoming a vice president at Brentwood, but that job was already taken by Dale Mathews, who was also a good friend. I didn't see Dale going anywhere for the foreseeable future. And I couldn't blame him. He was settled, and things were going well for him and pretty much everyone at Brentwood Music in those days. Plus, in 1993, Jim sold Brentwood Music to Zomba Music Group, creating a pivotal event in Brentwood's history. This change – at least in my mind – made the future at Brentwood Music for me (or anyone, for that matter) different than it had been at least and uncertain at most.

That hunch eventually proved to be true because although – as new owners always say – things would "stay the same," they didn't. Over the years, Brentwood Music got sliced and diced into several companies so that today, *none* of it exists any more as a free-standing corporate entity as it once did.

Founded independently in the mid-seventies by Clive Calder and Ralph Simon, Zomba had interests in music release, distribution, production, publishing, equipment rental, recording studios, and artist management. At the time, Zomba was widely regarded as the most successful of the independent music companies.

Zomba was probably best known for its role in developing some of the most popular forms of music, such as hip-hop in the 1980s and the teen pop/boy band phenomenon in the late 1990s through its first record label Jive. Zomba brought acts such as the Back Street Boys and Brittany Spears to the forefront.

Between my ambition for bigger and better things and Zomba's ultimate control over Brentwood, I saw the proverbial handwriting start to appear on the wall for me.

INTERMISSION WITH KITTY

The Broadway show was a hit. It was shoulder-to-shoulder in the Palace Theatre lobby at intermission, and the room was filled with the exciting energy that accompanies a new Broadway show when everyone knows they're watching something special. The show was *The Will Rogers Follies*, a new musical I was seeing on a business trip to New York City with Jim Van Hook. It starred Keith Carradine in the title role. Jim and I were standing in the lobby of the Palace Theatre when I spied – standing about ten feet from me – none other than Kitty Carlisle Hart.

"Jim, do you see who's standing over there? That's Kitty Carlisle Hart."

"Who?" said Jim.

"Kitty Carlisle Hart! She's walking Broadway history."

"Well, you should walk up to that walking history and introduce yourself," he replied.

"No way. I'm not going to interrupt Kitty Carlisle Hart while she's holding court," I protested.

"C'mon. You'll regret it if you don't," said the always wise Jim.

I pondered Jim's challenge for about three seconds. Then I made a beeline for Kitty.

At this point in the story, if this were a made-for-TV movie, the screen would blur and we would flash back to Kitty Carlisle's illustrious background. So envision the blur for a few seconds as you learn (or are reminded) about Mrs. Carlisle (even though her official last name was Hart, everyone always referred to her as Kitty Carlisle).

Irrepressible, witty, and smart, Kitty is best remembered as a regular panelist on the television game show *To Tell the Truth*. Known also for her gracious manners and personal elegance, Carlisle became prominent in New York City social circles as she crusaded for financial support of the arts. She served twenty years on the New York State Council on the Arts. In 1991, she received the National Medal of Arts from President George H. W. Bush.

Her family was of German Jewish heritage. Her mother was a woman obsessed with breaking into the prevailing Gentile society. (She once said to a taxi driver who asked if her daughter were Jewish, "She may be, but I'm not.") Carlisle's early education took place in New Orleans. In 1921, she was taken to Europe, where her mother hoped to marry her off to European royalty, believing the nobility there more amenable to a Jewish bride — only to end up flitting around Europe and living in what Carlisle recalled as "the worst room of the best hotel." Carlisle was educated at the Chateau Mont-Choisi in Lausanne, Switzerland, then at the Sorbonne and the London School of Economics. She studied acting in London at the Royal Academy of Dramatic Art.

After returning to New York in 1932 with her mother, she appeared on Broadway in several operettas and musicals and in the American premiere of Benjamin Britten's *The Rape of Lucretia*. She also sang the title role in Georges Bizet's *Carmen* in Salt Lake City. Carlisle's early movies included *Murder at the Vanities* (1934), *A Night at the Opera* (1935) with the Marx Brothers, and two films with Bing Crosby: *She Loves Me Not* (1934) and *Here Is My Heart* (1934).

Carlisle resumed her film career later in life, appearing in Woody Allen's *Radio Days* (1987) and in *Six Degrees of Separation* (1993), as well as on stage in a revival of *On Your Toes*. Her last movie appearance was in

Catch Me If You Can (2002) in which she played herself in a dramatization of a 1970s *To Tell the Truth* episode.

Carlisle became a household name through *To Tell the Truth*, where she was a regular panelist from 1956 to 1978, and later appeared on revivals of the series in 1980, 1990–91 and one episode in 2000. She was also a semi-regular panelist on *Password*, *Match Game*, *Missing Links*, and *What's My Line?*

She also widely performed her one-woman show in which she told anecdotes about the many great men in American musical theatre history whom she had personally known, notably George Gershwin, who had proposed marriage (according to an interview in *American Heritage* magazine), Irving Berlin, Kurt Weill, Oscar Hammerstein, Alan Jay Lerner, and Frederick Loewe. She interspersed her anecdotes with a few of the songs that made each of them famous. (Now *that* would have been a fun evening.)

I am told that Kitty decorated her sprawling Park Avenue duplex with a half-century of theatrical mementos, including posters featuring the prolific output of her husband, Moss Hart. The director of *My Fair Lady* and *Camelot*, he also co-wrote with George S. Kaufman the plays *You Can't Take It with You* and *Merrily We Roll Along* and collaborated with Cole Porter and Irving Berlin on hit musicals. (I was actually in our high school production of the Kaufman-Hart play *George Washington Slept Here*.)

Kitty married Moss in 1946. They were married only fifteen years, until his death of a heart attack at the age of fifty-seven. Together, they became a stylish, rags-to-riches Broadway couple, who found hard-fought happiness together.

Given that Kitty was only fifty-one when she was widowed, surely she must have had many opportunities to remarry. When asked that question later in life, she replied, "Oh, yes. But I loved Moss more than any beau I've ever had."

And now, I was approaching this "walking Broadway history."

As I came to the circle of friends who surrounded her, she saw me and I smiled. She graciously smiled at me, and then there was a pause in the conversation.

I said, "Mrs. Carlisle, I hope you'll forgive me for interrupting, but I couldn't help noticing you. It's wonderful to see you tonight looking as radiant as ever." And I meant every word of it.

Her smile turned into an even warmer smile, and she extended her hand as I introduced myself.

"I'm delighted to meet you, Mark." And she proceeded to introduce me to those around her.

"Are you enjoying the show?" I asked.

"It's simply fabulous. I think Cy [Coleman], Betty [Comden], and Adolph [Green] have a hit on their hands."

I couldn't resist evoking you-know-who's name before I slipped back to my comfortable spot in the lobby.

"What would Moss have thought about it?"

She laughed a hearty laugh and said, "Oh, I never predicted what Moss might have said. He was quite an original as I'm sure you know!"

With that, I smiled, asked forgiveness once again for the interruption, and politely exited.

After Kitty Carlisle Hart died in April 2007, her friends and admirers gathered at the Majestic Theatre on Broadway to pay tribute to such a legend. Her long-time piano accompanist played a Gershwin song and then turned to the audience to recall what Kitty had once told him about that melody: "When I die, I want you to play 'The Man I Love' in my key at the memorial service, and if I don't walk out on that stage you'll know I'm dead."

There was an eerie pause, a moment of silence, and then laughter and applause. The man she loved was long gone, and now, the keeper of his flame was also gone.

HERE'S DOC! (AND JOHNNY)

Ed McMahon stood six feet away from me. He had just completed warming up the audience for a taping of *The Tonight Show with Johnny Carson*.

"Five – four – three – two… ," said the stage manager, ticking off each number with his fingers. The last number was silent, and then he pointed at Ed. The NBC Orchestra kicked in to high gear, playing the classic theme song, led by the flamboyantly dressed hotshot trumpet player-conductor Doc Severinsen. And then, Ed's booming voice filled Studio 3 at NBC-TV in Burbank, California:

"Frooooom Hollywood…The Tonight Show starring Johnny Carson. This is Ed McMahon along with Doc Severinsen and the NBC Orchestra…"

I was on a trip to Los Angeles in the late 1980s. Ronald Reagan was in the White House, a gallon of gas cost $1.08, and The King of Late Night was still on his throne. And thanks to meeting Doc Severinsen a few years earlier, I had gotten a ticket to see *The Tonight Show with Johnny Carson* in person.

In preparation to write this chapter, I found my *Best of Johnny Carson* DVD set and watched about half an hour of clips from *The Tonight Show*. Remembering the Carson-era Tonight Show is like returning to the Golden

Age of television, and watching those clips from Carson's brand of late-night television back in the 1960s through the 1990s made me nostalgic for the kinder, gentler (and classier) host Johnny was.

Quite possibly the biggest star that television has ever produced, Carson commanded at his peak a nightly audience of fifteen million viewers – triple the current audience of any late night show combined. For those readers who don't remember Johnny Carson, I encourage some YouTube time with him. In my opinion, *The Tonight Show* has never been and will never be the same without Johnny. For thirty years, Johnny tucked America into bed each evening with his Midwestern mix of charm and cool. Ed McMahon was his announcer on his right, and Doc Severinsen was his bandleader on his left. And all was right with the world of late-night television.

It was three years before that night in NBC's Studio 3 watching Johnny Carson work his magic that I first met Doc Severinsen. I was in graduate school at the University of Tennessee and working as a roving reporter for WUTK-FM, the university's radio station. Since I had a degree in music, the station manager often had me cover music-related events that happened in Knoxville. So when it was announced that Doc Severinsen, Johnny Carson's celebrity trumpet-playing bandleader from *The Tonight Show*, was coming to UT for a concert, I got the assignment to cover him (!). Being a trumpet player myself only heightened my anticipation. My high school friend Ginny Thompson (who was also at the University of Tennessee in grad school by then) was giddy with excitement right along with me and accompanied me to the concert.

I was given a backstage pass, and prior to the concert, I was ushered into the Green Room to meet Doc. (The Green Room is whatever room the performers relax in prior to going on stage...be it Broadway or a college auditorium.) I walked into the room with my recording equipment, microphone, and questions.

I introduced myself, and Doc smiled a broad smile and extended his hand, instantly putting me at ease.

"Welcome, Mark. It's nice to meet you. I understand you work for the university's radio station," he said. "I'm ready to rock and roll."

After setting up my recording equipment I asked him the first question that was on my mind. Of course, I had done some advance research and had read his real first name was Carl, not Doc.

"So Doc is your nickname. How did you get it?" I asked.

"Well, my father was a dentist, and somewhere early in life my friends started calling me 'Little Doc.' When I grew up and wasn't little anymore, I was just 'Doc.' So it stuck and I've been Doc ever since."

I immediately shifted to *The Tonight Show*, which was at its zenith at the time. By then, Doc had been the show's bandleader for almost twenty years. How did he get his start on the show?

"Back in 1952 during Steve Allen's tenure as host of *The Tonight Show*, I occasionally played first trumpet in the band directed by Skitch Henderson. Later, I actually joined *The Tonight Show* Band several months before Johnny Carson became host in October 1962. I became the leader in 1967."

Under Severinsen's direction, *The Tonight Show* NBC Orchestra became the most visible big band in America. The band played incidental music for sketch comedy, guest introductions, and intermission music during station breaks. Severinsen took the opportunity to update many well-known swing music and jazz standards, including classics by Cole Porter, Dizzy Gillespie, and others.

Adept at comic bantering, Severinsen occasionally substituted for Ed McMahon as Johnny Carson's announcer and sidekick. Severinsen campaigned for the band to get featured slots during the show. The show introduced a "Stump the Band" segment in which audience members challenged the band to play obscure song titles, with the band responding with a comic piece.

"What are some of your favorite moments on the show?" I asked.

"Of course, doing special features with the band is great. And it's always funny whenever animals come on the show," he added. "Like the time Joan

Embery brought a python on the show, and it wrapped its tail around Johnny's crotch. The audience went wild."

"There have been so many incredible guests on the show over the years. Who are some of Johnny's favorite guests?" I had to know.

"He always enjoys Bob Newhart. They both come from the Midwest and have a lot in common. He also gets a kick out of Don Rickles. The list could go on…Angie Dickinson, Shelley Winters, Michael Landon…"

"What's Johnny like when the cameras aren't on?" I couldn't resist asking.

"Shy. He really isn't comfortable in social settings at all. But put him in front of an audience when the cameras turn on, and he's the King of Comedy," he said.

We wrapped up our time together, and Doc proceeded to give a knockout concert to a packed and appreciative audience.

Fast-forward to about three years later when I was on a trip to Los Angeles. I used my favorite friend, the phone, to see if I could get through to "Little Doc." After some twists and turns, I got his assistant on the phone. I relayed the story to her of the interview I'd conducted with Doc a few years before and wondered if it would be possible to get me in to see a taping of *The Tonight Show*. She said she would see what she could do after chatting with Doc.

I arrived at the NBC studios later that week, hoping there would be a ticket awaiting me to see the show that night. Sure enough, Doc took care of me and had a ticket with my name on it. Seeing Johnny Carson in action live – along with Ed and Doc and his band – is something I'll remember always. They just don't make television shows like that anymore.

Carson retired from show business on May 22, 1992, at age sixty-six, when he stepped down as host of *The Tonight Show*. His farewell was a major media event and stretched over several nights. Of course, Doc was on Johnny's left, just as he had been for many years, leading the band through that last historic show.

January 23, 2005, the world mourned when Johnny Carson died at

Cedars-Sinai Medical Center in West Hollywood of respiratory failure arising from emphysema. And the mantle as "King of Late Night" has never clearly passed to another.

Doc Severinsen is still performing on a regular basis with the group Doc Severinsen & the San Miguel 5. The group plays an eclectic variety of styles, including classical Spanish, gypsy jazz, and Latin and American ballads.

"Little Doc" is still going strong. And so do the memories for millions whom Johnny tucked into bed for those thirty years.

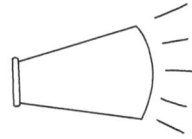

WAIT, WAIT... THERE'S MORE!

Go to www.docseverinsen.com or www.johnnycarson.com to see video clips and photos and learn more about these classic entertainers.

THE NORMAN CONQUEST

And now, I take you back to a time when dinosaurs roamed the earth and molten lava flowed freely. That's right…let's go back to the days when I was in college.

I was a senior at Mars Hill College (now Mars Hill University), and it was the annual Choral Festival time. What that means is that more than three hundred (auditioned) high school singers from North Carolina and some surrounding states converged on Mars Hill's campus to participate in a two-day festival and workshop, led by an all-star choral conductor. The festival culminated in a public performance of great choral music. I actually sang in the event twice while in high school (and it was this event that convinced me to choose Mars Hill to continue my education). As of this writing, the festival recently celebrated its 75th anniversary, so it has an incredible history.

That year's all-star leader of the Choral Festival was to be none other than the great Norman Luboff. Just who was he?

Born in Chicago in 1917, Norman Luboff studied at the University of Chicago and Central College in Chicago. Following this, he did graduate work with famed composer Leo Sowerby while singing and writing for radio programs in Chicago.

With a call from Hollywood to be choral director of *The Railroad Hour*, a radio weekly starring Gordon MacRae, Luboff began a successful career scoring numerous television programs and more than eighty motion pictures. He also recorded with artists such as Bing Crosby, Frank Sinatra, Jo Stafford, Frankie Laine, and Doris Day.

In 1950, he established Walton Music Corporation to publish his music. Luboff provided a vehicle for composers in Sweden to have their works available in the United States, including Egil Hovland and Waldemar Ahlen. Walton Music continues today as a major choral music publisher but is now owned by GIA Publications. Before it was sold to GIA, it was led by Luboff's widow, Gunilla Luboff, a former Swedish television producer.

Luboff was the founder and conductor of the Norman Luboff Choir, one of the leading choral groups of the fifties, sixties, and seventies. The choral group toured yearly from 1963 to 1987 and recorded more than seventy-five albums. The holiday albums *Songs of Christmas* (1956) and *Christmas with the Norman Luboff Choir* (1964) were perennial bestsellers for years. Luboff and his choir won the 1961 Grammy Award for Best Performance by a Chorus.

Luboff was a guest conductor at many choirs in the United States and abroad. And he was now coming to Mars Hill to guest conduct the festival. Anticipation was alive in that fresh Mars Hill mountain air.

Dr. Bill Thomas, then head of the choral department, asked me to join him in his office one day after choir rehearsal.

"Mark, as you know, Norman Luboff is coming next week, along with his wife, Gunilla, and I would like for you to be their personal guide and assistant during their stay," said Bill (or "BT" as we students called him).

"That's great, BT!" Thank you. What an honor!" said I in my callow, twenty-one-year-old voice.

BT explained that I was to pick up Mr. and Mrs. Luboff from the airport, make sure they got to their room, chauffeur them to all the rehearsals, and eat all their meals with them, while helping make their experience at Mars Hill enjoyable overall. I was delighted. I would get to hang out with a legend.

And sure enough, the next week, there I was hanging with Norman and Gunilla. At well over six feet and built strongly, Norman was somewhat of an imposing physical presence. He had a booming voice to match and a studied, serious manner. Gunilla was very pleasant and warm. As noted earlier, she had been a broadcaster in Sweden so she was a natural conversationalist.

I did my duties for them gladly, learning things about Norman's music publishing business along the way through questions I asked him. Even then, I was fascinated with the music business in general and print music publishing specifically.

Finally, at dinner on the night of the big concert, Norman looked at me squarely in the eye and addressed me by name for the first time since meeting him. "Mark," he said in that big, booming voice.

"Yes, sir?" I said, again in my callow, twenty-one-year-old voice, which seemed even callower as I responded to this legend.

"I need for you to pick up Gunilla and me from our room before the concert and drive us to the concert hall."

With my tail wagging and coat shining, I said eagerly, "Why, of course, Mr. Luboff. I will be more than happy to do that."

We wrapped up dinner and I bid them farewell. They went to their room where they prepared and dressed for the concert, which he would conduct. Meanwhile, I went to the auditorium where the concert was to take place later that evening. Our college choir was to sing as well (under Norman's direction), and we had a quick rehearsal in preparation.

Since I was dining with the Luboffs, I was slightly late getting to the rehearsal. That didn't sit well with the choir president (a fellow student), and he let me know it immediately. Being late to a rehearsal at Mars Hill was simply unacceptable. Of course, I knew that but thought it would be rude for me to skip out and leave the Luboffs all alone at dinner. In any event, the sum total of the episode was that it knocked me off my game.

However, the concert soon got successfully under way, and I was standing in the choir while BT conducted. We finished the second number, and

BT whirled around to the audience to announce our distinguished guest conductor for the evening. "Ladies and gentlemen, it gives me great pleasure to introduce our guest conductor. He's a world-renowned…."

I think I must have blacked out right after I heard "world-renowned" because I do not remember BT saying anything else after that. I was immediately struck with terror because I realized: *I forgot to pick up Norman Luboff. And Gunilla.*

The *one thing* he had directly asked me to do for him the entire weekend, and *I blew it*. I blew it. As Meredith Willson would say, I laid an egg. (Come to think of it, I'll bet Norman and Meredith probably knew each other.)

As I stood there, BT's introduction seemed to last a lifetime. I'm sure it was in actuality a very appropriate length to introduce this legend, but every word BT said about Norman seemed to hang in the air like a knife over my head. "Legendary. Brilliant. Talented," said BT.

And thanks to me, *absent*.

Who knew? He was possibly in a ditch somewhere cursing my name even as I stood there. And there would be Gunilla by his side, pleasant as ever. Or maybe she had turned on me too. I couldn't blame her. I could see her Swedish blonde hair caked in mud since she had certainly fallen down the side of one of those mountains as they tried to make their way to the concert that night. Yes, and surely there would be a lawsuit.

It's amazing how such moments can seem to last forever. The sweat was starting to run down my temples.

Finally, BT came to the end of his introduction. I just knew the minute Luboff didn't appear at the podium, the entire earth would open up and swallow me like a giant choral music sinkhole and carry me off to the Gates of Hell where I belonged.

"Ladies and gentlemen, Norman Luboff!"

Thunderous applause from a few thousand people in the audience.

But no Norman.

Again, BT wound up and pitched the ball.

"Ladies and gentlemen, Norman Luboff!"

The applause returned, but it was somehow more tentative, as if you could hear the audience thinking, *Where is he?*

Again, seconds passed like hours. I was planning what I would do since inevitably BT and the rest of the Mars Hill music faculty, administration, custodians, local farm animals, my cousins, and my immediate family would prevent me from graduating. In those moments, I bargained with God in every form imaginable. If God would allow Norman Luboff to magically appear (*a deus ex machina*, as it were), I would never, ever commit another sin for the rest of my life. Period. Plus, no more sweets. Whatever it took, I was willing to do it.

Finally, and I mean *finally*, Norman Luboff came shuffling up to the podium, looking slightly disheveled.

There is a God, I thought. *But I'll bet He is upset too.*

I wiped the sweat off my brow and lifted my folder to sing the piece of Norman Luboff music he had written and was now to conduct. And every time he cued the tenors, *he looked straight at me.*

But how did he get to the concert? Hitchhike? Catch a bus? Buy a car? Take a taxi? Magic carpet? Frankly, I didn't care at that moment. I was just so dang thankful that it looked like I would graduate from college after all.

After the concert was over, I rushed up to him, apologizing for the error. I started speaking his name ten feet before I got to him.

"Mr. Luboff…Mr. Luboff…," I said breathlessly.

"Mark, don't worry, don't worry," he said, smiling.

He was smiling!

"But how…"

He didn't let me finish.

And then two words tumbled out of his mouth that I'll never forget: "We walked."

OMG (as we say in texts and e-mails these days). The Great Norman Luboff and Gunilla *walked* to the concert! All because of me!

And there was no mud in Gunilla's hair.

Fortunately, however, truth be told, it was only about a five-minute walk. *But still…*

The following morning, I redeemed myself (I hope) when I drove Norman and Gunilla to the airport at a very early hour. I practically stayed up all night so I would make sure I didn't oversleep.

And now, we fast-forward to some twenty years later. I was in the music publishing business and working at Hal Leonard Corporation, which had just landed the distribution deal for the Walton Music publishing company (the aforementioned company Norman had founded in 1950). By now, Norman had passed away, and his widow, Gunilla, was running it. I was asked to sit in a meeting with Gunilla, who had come to town for the usual meetings in such circumstances.

I entered the room confidently where Gunilla was already seated with several others from Hal Leonard. Surely, she would never remember me.

"How nice to meet you, Gunilla. I'm Mark…"

She didn't let me finish.

"Oh yes, oh yes," she said in her beautiful Swedish accent. "I remember you well, Mark."

Suddenly, I was back in that concert standing with my choir folder waiting for Norman to show up as my life flashed before me. Could Mars Hill take away my degree at this point?

"You're the one who forgot Norman and me!" she said.

"Well, I, uh, I, well…" My words turned to ashes.

"Norman went to his grave never forgetting that terrible experience," Gunilla said.

Now, I was turning seven shades of red and needing oxygen. "I'm so sorry to hear…," I said, trying to ease her evident pain.

But she could stand it no longer. She burst into laughter, along with the rest of the room. One of the Hal Leonard people present knew my Norman Luboff story and prepped Gunilla prior to her visit with me.

Gunilla told me that she didn't remember me forgetting Norman and her or even the visit to Mars Hill, for that matter. She and Norman did so many concerts and festivals together back in those days, they were all a blur. In the years to come, Gunilla and I became good friends because of our work together in the music publishing business.

If that weren't enough, Norman's son, Pete, and his wife, Pat, are big-time hit songwriters who moved to Nashville from Los Angeles several years ago. Through Gunilla, I met them, and we've become great friends (and co-writers) as well.

Pete and Pat wrote a very successful book titled *88 Songwriting Wrongs and How to Right Them*. I asked them to inscribe it for me. They did so and wrote:

"Dear Mark: Although you forgot Norman and Gunilla, we will never forget you."

Well, Pete and Pat, if something knocks me off my game again, you'd better not ask me to take you to an important event (unless you want some exercise).

PRELUDE TO THE PRESS

It was snowing lightly in Shelby, North Carolina, and Mrs. Haworth, my sixth grade chorus teacher, raised her hands to conduct the closing song at our Christmas concert.

The auditorium was packed with parents (including my own) and others, and the song we sang was the hit of the concert. It was the Christmas classic "Do You Hear What I Hear?" I noticed it was published by Shawnee Press, Inc., located in a town that sounded mystical and foreign to a little sixth grade chorus boy. The town was named Delaware Water Gap, Pennsylvania.

So what makes an eleven-year-old kid notice not only who published a piece of music but also where the publisher is located?

That, my friend, helps make the world go 'round (oh, and also love).

By the time I reached college I had sung or conducted a truckload of Shawnee Press chorals, as well as played dozens of Shawnee band or solo arrangements as a trumpet player. I became attached to Shawnee Press and the type and quality of music it produced. I paid close attention to the actual layout of the music, let alone the content. I can even remember at one point while in high school taking out a map of Pennsylvania, finding Delaware Water Gap on that map, and telling some friends that I wanted to work for Shawnee Press someday.

In the summer I graduated from high school, I orchestrated a Shawnee Press children's musical (*Tom Sawyer*) for a summer drama program the public school system staged that year. The following summer, I musically directed and again orchestrated another Shawnee Press elementary musical (*The Prince and the Pauper*) for that same summer drama program. I actually had the nerve to send my orchestration for *Tom Sawyer* to Shawnee in hopes of getting it published. No such luck, but the company sent a gentle and encouraging rejection letter to me. So my connection with Shawnee Press was significant and fond.

During my junior year in college, when a few friends and I impulsively decided to take a road trip to New York City (my first time ever to NYC), I insisted we stop at Shawnee Press on the way home. It was sort of on the way, and they agreed to humor me.

When we drove into Delaware Water Gap that quiet Sunday afternoon, I found a sleepy, yet charming, community. So *this* was the community where Shawnee Press was located! Suddenly, I was in the sixth grade chorus all over again.

Delaware Water Gap is situated in the heart of the Pocono Mountains, where people often vacation or have summer homes. The Delaware Water Gap is on the border of New Jersey and Pennsylvania where the Delaware River cuts through a large ridge of the Appalachian Mountains—creating a "water gap" – hence the name of the community. Since this was pre-MapQuest or GPS, we had to stop at a local gas station to find out where Shawnee Press was located. As we drove up the hill on the main street of that little town, my anticipation was in overdrive. Finally, there it was on the left side of the street! Shawnee Press! And it was…

A dump.

Well, not a total dump. It was just a very old building (buildings, actually), which had obviously seen better days. Little did I know of the rich history of the old buildings, known as the Castle Inn. This was my first lesson that music publishers needn't be in impressive buildings or locations to get the job done.

But nevertheless, there it was – Shawnee Press. *Home at last*, I thought. Twenty-four years later, this community would indeed be my home for a brief time. Here was where all those incredible music arrangements sung or played by millions over the years had been created by the legendary likes of Hawley Ades, Roy Ringwald, Luigi Zaninelli, and many more. I had become such a Shawnee Press aficionado in high school, some of my friends had nicknamed me "Hawley Ades." (Years later, when I met Hawley – who was in his nineties by then– I told him that story, and he roared with laughter. I found Hawley to be a gentle and kind person, and his talent as an arranger in his heyday was unparalleled.)

Shawnee Press was founded in 1939 by famed bandleader-choirmaster from the Golden Age of radio and television, Fred Waring. Waring and his famous singing group The Pennsylvanians achieved national prominence on radio and television in the 1930s through the 1970s. In my opinion, Fred Waring was poised to become more popular than Lawrence Welk, but I was told he didn't like the grind and high-maintenance production of television, and he shied away from a long-term television schedule.

As Fred and The Pennsylvanians grew in popularity, school and church choral directors began requesting copies of Waring's unique arrangements, and Waring responded by starting a music publisher based in New York City. Originally named "Words and Music" the new venture included Jack Benny as one of the original investors along with Waring. Waring eventually bought out the other investors and moved the company to his native Pennsylvania, eighty miles outside New York City to Shawnee On Delaware (and eventually Delaware Water Gap). Accordingly, he changed the name of the company from "Words and Music" to "Shawnee Press."

Thanks to Waring's reputation and vast contacts, Shawnee had become *the* pop music choral publisher in the 1960s and 1970s. The company controlled print rights to the major current pop songs at that time as well as the classic ones (everything from Lennon and McCartney to Gershwin and Porter). The company also published band, orchestra, solo, and ensemble music as well as music for elementary schools. In addition, the company had entered the church market in the 1960s with the acquisition of a church music catalog named Harold Flammer (hmmm…wonder what the name of the founder of that company was?). In the 1970s, thanks to the leadership of expert and amazing Shawnee choral editor Lew Kirby, the company deepened its commitment to church music when Lew founded another church music imprint, which he called GlorySound. It was targeted to the growing contemporary Christian music movement. The sum total of all of this was that Shawnee had become a force to be reckoned with as an educational music publisher and clearly the number one publisher of that type of music at the time.

Then Fred Waring started to get older (funny how that happens) and more interested in other things. Fred had financed the patent for the first electric blender (of all things), for which he proceeded to make loads of money. Entire books have been written on Fred Waring's amazing career, so I'm not about to attempt to recount it here. And although those who knew Fred best didn't always speak highly of him personally (he was quite the taskmaster), they most always spoke respectfully. According to those closest to him, he was a demanding perfectionist and could be exasperating. But there were many to whom he was beloved.

Back in the 1960s, Fred had hired the very talented couple of Ernest and Marjorie Farmer to work at Shawnee Press. I knew their names well. Ernie became Shawnee's president, taking care of day-to-day operations, and Marjorie was a choral editor. Fred and Ernie got along well enough, but Fred and Marjorie never hit it off.

By the early 1980s, Ernie had become legendary in the music business in his own right, serving on the ASCAP Board of Directors and in other key industry roles, in addition to running Shawnee Press. Marjorie was turning out superb work as an editor and writer for Shawnee that was selling well. But Fred Waring Jr. was waiting in the wings, and Fred Sr. had just about had his fill of Marjorie (and probably vice versa).

According to a personal conversation I had years later with Ernie, he told me he came into work one day, and there were literally pink slips of paper in his and Marjorie's mailboxes at the office. After decades with Shawnee Press, he and Marjorie were being summarily fired on the spot with nothing more than pink slips in their mailboxes. They were to clean out their offices and be gone immediately. Ernie and Marjorie were not pleased, to say the least, not only about being fired but also about how it was handled.

However, they soon got busy and—with a certain amount of revenge – started their own music publisher right up the street from Shawnee and called it Wide World Music. They published the exact same material as Shawnee and did quite well. Eventually, Marjorie's health failed, and as she and Ernie got older, they sold the company to Shawnee Press.

The full circle was completed. Ernie and Marjorie retired to the sun and warmer climes of Arizona. (When I spoke to Ernie on a few occasions after meeting him many years later, I could tell that fateful ending to his and Marjorie's careers at Shawnee still evoked ill feelings. And I couldn't blame him, given the circumstances he described to me.)

Meanwhile, Fred Waring Jr. took over Shawnee Press when Ernie and Marjorie were fired. Although I never had the pleasure of meeting Fred Jr., I did hear stories of his tenure at the company. I'm sure there were some triumphs, but according to those who were Shawnee employees during the period, he presided over the company's decline. Other publishers easily took advantage of Shawnee's growing weaknesses. A certain music publisher in Milwaukee (Hal Leonard Corporation) was becoming very aggressive in the pop music area at that time and scooped up the pop copyright print contracts from Shawnee. Also, Shawnee had a long-standing agreement with Warner Brothers (which included the famed Warner-Chappell catalog, containing top pop and Broadway songs) to produce printed arrangements of their songs. As Shawnee continued to weaken, Warner decided to get into the then lucrative print music business on its own and created Warner Brothers Publications (dissolving its prior agreement with Shawnee), thus shutting Shawnee out of putting those top pop songs into print.

The pop music doors that had been a vital part of Shawnee's revenues for so long were now closing. However, church music continued to grow at Shawnee under Lew Kirby's leadership. Accordingly, sacred music soon became the tail that wagged the proverbial dog for the company out of necessity. (I eventually met Lew Kirby, who became a dear friend. Of all the church music editors I've known over the years, I put Lew at the top of the list for his expert editorial and producing skills.)

Eventually, it was time to face the music. In an attempt to save Shawnee, Fred Waring Sr. stepped back in and fired his son. His action created a lot of nasty publicity for the company. After his firing –as the urban legend is told – Fred Jr. set up a hot dog stand in Delaware Water Gap in order to humiliate and embarrass his father. Fred Sr. then became a bit more hands-on with Shawnee for a short season, but in 1984 he suffered a massive heart attack at Penn State the morning after a music workshop he had led. The era of Fred Waring had come to an abrupt end.

Enter Virginia Waring, Fred's widow.

Virginia (*nee* Morley) Waring stepped in out of necessity to run Shawnee Press upon Fred's unexpected death. She was a brilliantly talented concert pianist who met Fred through her work on his radio show. She was an elegant lady and a very savvy one at that. (I became friends with Virginia years later in my role with Shawnee and found her to be absolutely charming, witty, and very smart.) But Virginia ultimately didn't know enough about running a music publisher and was smart enough to realize that. Accordingly, she soon tapped Ruth Sibley to serve as VP-CEO of Shawnee. Ruth had been Fred Waring's personal assistant and right hand for a long time, and she knew Fred very well. Ruth had some great stories about him and the early days of Shawnee Press. She also had a great deal of respect for "FW" or "Mr. Waring," as she often referred to him. And she knew the Shawnee catalog well and was widely loved by the staff. Ruth ran Shawnee for ten years until Virginia decided it was in her best interest to sell Shawnee in 1989.

Enter Music Sales Corporation, a company based in England and owned by the eccentric and shrewd Bob Wise. Several people courted Virginia to buy Shawnee Press, but she hit it off with Music Sales President Barrie Edwards and therefore, she sold to them. Even though Barrie had no interest whatsoever in print music, Bob Wise loved it and wanted another notch in his belt. Besides, being the wise man (pun intended) he was, he knew the Shawnee catalog contained a very lucrative copyright: the music theme to the Olympic Games – yes, the Olympics of all things. Sure, there were several print music arrangements of the song that had been sold over the years, but that revenue was chump change compared to the television royalties (or synchronization rights, as they are called) that are garnered from such usages. Barrie once told me that Shawnee had been charging NBC-TV about $20,000 for usage of the theme, but when Music Sales acquired the catalog the price went up to more than $350,000. The NBC Peacock didn't blink, and NBC willingly paid it in order to keep using the classic theme song.

In 1994, while I was still at Brentwood Music, I met Ruth Sibley at a trade show, and we hit it off big, standing there in the Shawnee booth. I told her of my love of Shawnee Press since my grade school days and my pilgrimage to Shawnee while in college…all of which she enjoyed. She suggested we get together for coffee sometime during the trade show to continue our discussion. We did so, and she regaled me with incredible stories about the Fred Waring days. I loved hearing about those days – truly the Golden Era for Shawnee Press. But times had changed, and the 1960s were long gone. The people who knew of Fred Waring and his Pennsylvanians were either dead or in rest homes, by and large. Ruth was already into her seventies and was looking for someone to succeed her as head of Shawnee Press. She said she wanted it to be me.

After the trade show, we exchanged letters, which led to her flying me to Delaware Water Gap in Pennsylvania, where Shawnee was still based, and giving me a tour of the offices and community. It had been thirteen years since my first visit there. This time, I was not a callow college student but an invited guest by the head of Shawnee Press. The next step, she said, was for me to meet Barrie Edwards.

In a few short weeks, I found myself stepping off a plane at New York's La Guardia airport and taking a cab to the Music Sales corporate offices on

Park Avenue. I took the elevator up to the twentieth floor and was soon sitting in a conference room with Barrie Edwards.

Barrie is from Wales, so he has a distinct accent, which is very endearing to me. He was warm and cordial, but I could tell he seemed to be going through the motions just a bit. I had been in the music business only six years, and while that's not a terribly short time, it's not what I would call a wealth of experience. We talked about what I would do for Shawnee were I in charge, and I shared several ideas with him. Our meeting lasted about an hour, and then I was on my way back to Nashville and my job at Brentwood Music.

I eventually heard…nothing. At least not from Barrie, but Ruth called about a month later to tell me Barrie had decided to hire Lynn Sengstack as her successor. Seems someone else at Music Sales knew of Lynn and highly recommended her to Barrie before I met with him. I'd never heard of Lynn before but found out she was the daughter of the owner-president of a long-established music publishing company, Summy-Birchard, and had some management experience. So Lynn was hired as VP-CEO of Shawnee Press. At Barrie's suggestion, she reached out to me at a trade show to hear some of my ideas. We had a nice chat, but it was of little consequence. The door to Shawnee had closed to me. At least then. I went back to Nashville to continue my work at Brentwood Music.

Little did I know I would have more interactions with both Barrie and Lynn a decade later.

RODGERS, RODGERS AND HAMMERSTEIN

I put on a coat and walked out of my hotel room in New York City. I hadn't taken more than five steps toward the elevator when I remembered the weather forecast was calling for snow, and you don't want to be in New York City without an umbrella when it's snowing or raining. So I immediately turned around and went back to the room to fetch my umbrella.

As I walked through the door, the phone was ringing. I rushed over and answered.

"Is this Mark Cabaniss?" the voice asked on the other end.

"Yes, it is," I replied, still in full charge of my senses.

"Hi, Mark. This is Mary Rodgers," she said.

Incredible! I thought. Had I not come back for my umbrella, I would have missed the call I was hoping to receive. (This was clearly before the invention of cell phones).

Mary Rodgers is the daughter of famed composer Richard Rodgers, one-half of the immortal Rodgers and Hammerstein. From *The Sound of Music* to *South Pacific*; *Oklahoma!* to *The King and I* and *Cinderella*, this world-famous duo created some of the most enduring works in the American Musical Theatre canon.

But Mary Rodgers is a successful composer and author in her own right. Rodgers wrote the music for musicals and revues, including *Once Upon a Mattress* (which made a star out of Carol Burnett), *From A to Z*, *Hot Spot*, *The Mad Show*, *Working*, and Phyllis Newman's one-woman show *The Madwoman of Central Park West*. Of her work for *Once Upon a Mattress*, then *New York Times* critic Brooks Atkinson applauded Mary's "vigorous musical intelligence" and "musical richness."

Mary has also written children's books, most notably *Freaky Friday*, which was made into a feature film by Disney for which she also wrote the screenplay.

So how was it that I was picking up the phone that day and Mary Rodgers was asking to speak to me?

I was conducting the pit orchestra for a production of *South Pacific*, and one of the cast members, Sue, came to me and told me about the weekend she'd just had in New York City. Seems she was friends with well-known playwright Marsha Norman, who is friends with Mary Rodgers, and they'd all had dinner together. When Sue met Mary, she told her about the production of *South Pacific* she was currently rehearsing and how its conductor was a composer.

"I told Mary I'm sure you would enjoy meeting her, and she said she would be delighted to do so," said Sue.

That was the understatement of the year.

"I thought the next time you're in New York, I'll call Marsha and have her set it up for you to meet Mary," said Sue.

And of course, ever the one to follow up (especially in such a case), I let Sue know a few months later when a New York City trip developed for me. Sue phoned Marsha Norman about my upcoming trip. This was during the week of Christmas so things got busy as usual for everyone, and I never heard back from Sue whether Marsha was able to set up the meeting between Mary and me. I flew to New York on January 2 thinking the meeting wouldn't happen. And then the phone rang in my New York hotel room on that soon-to-be snowy afternoon. Thanks to the efforts of Sue and Marsha, Mary had magically tracked me down.

"Hi, Mary!" I said, with a mix of surprise and familiarity as if I had known her for years. Because, knowing her music, I felt as if I did.

After we chatted about how she was able to track me down, I asked if I could visit her while I was in the City to interview her for a radio program. She obliged and invited me to visit in her Central Park West apartment the following day.

When I walked into her beautiful and spacious apartment the next day, we went to the living room where I immediately noticed her grand piano. When we sat down, the piano was a natural segue to speak about her writing.

"I think writing music has an instant emotional impact on you as you're doing it," she said. "One note leads to the next...one chord leads to the next. I think I could write music for twenty hours a day and not be bored."

I instantly found Mary Rodgers to be gracious, graceful, and totally down to earth. After we chatted a bit more about writing in general, I couldn't wait to speak about *Once Upon a Mattress*.

"I played the part of the Minstrel in my hometown's community theatre production of *Mattress* several years ago," I said. "I fell in love with that show. How did it come about?"

"There was a summer camp resort in the Pocono Mountains in Pennsylvania called Camp Tamiment," she said. "Marshall Barer, Jay Thompson, and I were asked to do a show for the camp, and we decided to do a fun adaptation of *The Princess and the Pea* fairy tale. It was a one-act show that we wrote in three weeks. It was supposed to run for only a weekend. But it was such a hit, it was held over...and over. Some New York producers heard about it, came to see it, and asked us if we could expand the show to two acts. We immediately said, 'Yes,' hoping we could actually do it!

"The producers then asked us to audition the show for [legendary director] George Abbott. He agreed to direct if we could finish out the book and new songs. We had six weeks to get it finished," she said.

And get it finished they did. The result is the "true story" of *The Princess and the Pea*, a hilarious romp through medieval England, which tells the fairy tale through a colorful, tuneful, musical comedy lens.

Not only did George Abbott sign on after hearing the final draft of the show, but the producers also landed an up-and-coming television star named Carol Burnett.

"One of Carol's big dreams was that she would do a Broadway musical someday and wanted to work with George Abbott on it. That dream came true for Carol with our show," Mary said.

The Princess and the Pea became *Once Upon a Mattress* and opened at the Phoenix Theatre Off-Broadway in May 1959. Although overall critical reaction was mixed, audiences loved it (and critics were unanimous in their praise of Carol Burnett). Rodgers's score received high marks from many critics. The show was such a commercial hit that a transfer to Broadway happened later that year where the show went on to run for a solid 244 performances and received a Tony Award nomination. The Broadway run spawned a successful London production and three television movie versions over the years. The show has been a very popular choice for high schools and community theatres for decades.

"What was it like working with Carol Burnett?" I asked.

"She was a total delight," said Mary with a smile. "And also a complete professional. Making musicals comes with a lot of last minute changes during preview performances, and Carol never flinched at learning new songs and dialog on the spot," she added.

I could have spoken about *Mattress* for another hour, but I couldn't sit with the daughter of Richard Rodgers and not ask about her "daddy" as she calls him.

"I think Daddy was somewhat embarrassed about my writing at first," she said. "I was writing really terrible pop music and lyrics. But then I began writing children's songs. He listened to them and said, 'Those aren't so bad. Maybe you ought to keep that up.' From that point on, he was somewhat encouraging."

What was he like as a person?

"I think he was unhappy unless he was writing. That was what he loved to do. I think that's why he continued writing long after the point he actually should have. He eventually started to repeat himself. I don't think he ever really worked successfully with anyone after Oscar died," she said. "Some asked, 'Why doesn't he stop? He's got plenty of money.' And I said, 'Because that's the only way he's alive…when he's writing.'"

The Sound of Music – though not Rodgers and Hammerstein's most favorite of their collaborations (that was *Carousel*) – has certainly been by far the most commercially successful. What special memories did Mary have about *The Sound of Music*?

"During the Boston tryout of the show, Daddy felt Captain von Trapp should have a song with which he would bid farewell to the Austria he knew and loved. So Daddy wrote the music for 'Edelweiss' before Oscar had written the lyrics. That was a departure for them since Okie [Oscar] always wrote the lyrics first. But Okie was ill with cancer and got to Boston late. It's a lovely song."

She continued: " 'Edelweiss' was the last song that Rodgers and Hammerstein wrote together. Oscar's cancer took his life nine months after *The Sound of Music* opened on Broadway. He didn't live to see the immortal film version."

I knew our time was coming to a close, and as she saw me to the door, we looked at several of the family pictures on her piano. She told me about several people in the pictures, including one of her sons, Adam Guettel.

"Adam is quite a composer and lyricist," she said proudly. Little did I know that in the years to come, Adam would become famous as well for his very successful musical theatre creations such as *Floyd Collins* and *The Light in the Piazza* (for which he won two Tony Awards).

Three generations strong, the Rodgers creative DNA is obviously an amazing force to be reckoned with.

HELLO, UNCLE HAL

All my friends in Nashville warned me.

In late May of 1995, at the going away party that Jim Van Hook gave me when I announced I was leaving Brentwood Music, my friends warned me: "It gets really cold in Milwaukee."

Yes, it does. Forty degrees below zero cold at times. Not my idea of a good time.

I found that out firsthand. But before I moved to Milwaukee in 1995, let's rewind to 1993. It was there where the annual RPMDA (Retail Print Music Dealers Association) Convention was being held that year, and I was to attend in my capacity as head of Designer Music.

I was attending the opening convention gathering, and one of my industry friends introduced me to a man whom I'd never heard of nor met before, Keith Mardak. Keith was none other than the president of Hal Leonard Corporation ("Uncle Hal" to its employees), based in Milwaukee. Hal Leonard is the powerhouse print music publisher in the world. Keith is a brilliant businessman and a legend in the print music business. We exchanged the usual opening remarks, and our conversation soon turned to business. When Keith found out I was in the church music business, he wanted to know more.

"Have you ever done a Christian fake book?" asked Keith.

"No. When I hear the words 'Christian fake book' I think of evangelist Jim Bakker," I replied.

He gave me his business card. "Call me and let's talk about it," he said.

A fake book is a thick spiral-bound book with simple melody lines and chord symbols used by bands and other musicians for performing at a variety of occasions: nightclubs, weddings, and so on. There are fake books for various styles, such as pop, rock, country, and jazz. But until then, no one had produced a fake book with Christian songs.

Intrigued by the meeting with Mr. Mardak and always one to follow up, I took out his business card a few days after I'd returned to Nashville. I was continuing to grow wary of the changes that Zomba was implementing at Brentwood, and I felt that the Golden Age of Brentwood Music was starting to slip away.

So I called Keith Mardak. He told me he envisioned a Christian fake book that would be a joint venture between Hal Leonard and Brentwood Music. I liked the idea and took it to Jim. He liked it, too, but said he would need to contact Zomba to get their thoughts about doing a joint venture with another company. (Of course, prior to Jim's selling Brentwood, there would have been no need to run the idea past anyone else. If he had liked the idea, that would have been good enough.)

A few days later, Jim told me he'd been informed by Zomba they already had a print music deal in place with Warner Brothers Publications, located in Miami, and wanted me to approach them first with the idea. When I called Warner Brothers Publications to see if they had an interest in the idea, two of their top brass immediately booked a flight for later that week to Nashville to meet with us (Warner Brothers Publications was a big competitor of Hal Leonard, so they were always trying to one-up Hal Leonard).

The guys from Warner Brothers came to town, and a deal was struck. I had to call Keith to tell him the news. He was undaunted (typical of Keith, I found out after eventually getting to know him). He said, "The next time you're in Milwaukee, let's sit down and see what else we might do together."

Keith was determined to get Hal Leonard into the church music business one way or another. The company had tried – with no success – in previous years to publish church music.

So, once again, as the guy who always follows up, I devised a reason to go to Milwaukee in March of 1995. It was St. Patrick's Day and there I was in Milwaukee, sitting in Keith's spacious corner office at the Hal Leonard headquarters on West Bluemound Road.

I remember my exact words to him early in the conversation: "I think Hal Leonard can be successful in the church music business."

He was interested. I shared with him several ideas on how that could be achieved, through new marketing and product development directions.

He picked up his phone and made a few impromptu calls to his vice presidents, asking them about various numbers on current sales of the relatively small number of church music products they were currently selling.

He then gave me a tour of the building (an impressive operation), and as we parted he said, "The ball is in our court. We'll be in touch."

I received a call from Keith the next week. They were very interested in forging ahead on hiring me and moving me to Milwaukee to start the new Hal Leonard Church Music division. I was very excited about this new opportunity. We made an appointment for me to fly back to Milwaukee the following week to discuss salary and other particulars.

But before I said, "Hello," to Uncle Hal, there was another gentleman caller. This gentleman was named Don Hinshaw.

While I was in graduate school at the University of Tennessee, I had written my master's thesis on Hinshaw Music, located in Chapel Hill, North Carolina. I had been acquainted with the music published by Hinshaw since my undergraduate days and always had a great deal of respect for what they published.

Hinshaw Music was founded in 1975 by Don Hinshaw. Don had cut his teeth in the music business as a choral editor at the long-established firm of Carl Fischer (founded in 1872) in New York City. After some disagreements with upper management, Don moved back to his native North Carolina and started Hinshaw Music. The company had experienced rapid growth under his guidance and sharp editorial eye, and now, more than a decade after I'd met him and written my thesis on his company, I picked up the phone and there he was.

"Mark, I would like to fly you to Chapel Hill to discuss the future of Hinshaw Music," said Don. I was surprised and excited.

The next thing I knew I was on a plane to Raleigh and would spend the next two days talking to Don and his associates about possibly coming on board with Hinshaw Music. Don told me he wanted me to be his assistant so that he could train me, but he made it clear his intention was to have me succeed him as president of the company in the future.

It was a very nice meeting, but I told him I was in discussions with Hal Leonard. He was unfazed and said that Hal Leonard and Hinshaw Music presented two very different possible paths before me if I chose to leave Brentwood Music. And he was right. The two companies were – and are – very different.

I struggled with the decision at first, and as much as I liked Don and his publishing philosophy, I knew I had to move toward Hal Leonard. The opportunity to found a full church music division at a company such as Hal Leonard was irresistible.

Hal Leonard and I soon came to terms, and a few months later, I was moving to Milwaukee – fortunately in the warmth of spring. Things had moved fast. From making my first phone call to Keith Mardak to showing up in Milwaukee to report for work at Hal Leonard, only three months had transpired.

And a year and a half later, Don Hinshaw was dead. He suffered a heart attack while vacationing in Mexico. An important era in Hinshaw Music's history had passed.

I would spend the next ten years building the Hal Leonard church music division. It was a rewarding time in many ways, and I learned the ins and outs of Hal Leonard. It was an amazing company, but with a very buttoned-down and prescribed corporate culture (which has obviously worked well for the company over the long years).

I was into my sixth year in Milwaukee, and although I had become very involved in a local church there and made wonderful friends, I didn't want to remain in the cold Midwest for the rest of my life. I missed Nashville, that region of the country, and its proximity to my past and all the people associated with it. And yet, I was happy overall with my job at Hal Leonard. But something had to give.

The winds of change started to blow when I received an offer to become a church music director in Nashville. Although the job offer somewhat interested me, what attracted me the most was the prospect of getting back to Nashville.

By then, Keith Mardak had promoted Larry Morton to the position of president of Hal Leonard (and Keith became chairman/CEO). Larry Morton had come up through the ranks of Hal Leonard and made a truckload of friends and fans along the way (for good reason). He is very bright, a hard worker, and extremely smart in regard to the music business and to life in general. And he is a warm and genuinely caring person. He was consistently a champion of mine during my entire tenure at Hal Leonard and became a dear and close business associate and friend.

I asked Larry to have lunch with me. We went to a small Italian restaurant where we often had lunch when we wanted privacy to discuss business.

"I've been offered a job in Nashville and I'm seriously considering taking it," I told him.

"Really? That's big news," said Larry, looking somewhat taken aback.

I proceeded to give him more details, and he listened carefully. I told him I had a choice to make: stay in Milwaukee or move back to Nashville. I explained why I wanted to move back to Nashville.

"Why couldn't you do your job for us from Nashville?" he asked.

I was stunned. In the far recesses of the back of my mind I had hoped he might say such a thing, but I figured he wouldn't go there. As I said before,

Hal Leonard's culture is very prescribed and allows little room for such an idea of an employee working from home in another city.

"I would love that," I said. "That would be the best of both worlds."

Over the next few weeks, Larry and I worked out the details of a move for me and discussed the plan of my eventually hiring an editorial assistant and possibly a few local telesales reps to focus on the continued growing Hal Leonard Church Music Division. It was an exciting picture.

By February of the following year, with twenty-seven inches of snow on the ground in Milwaukee, I drove out of town into the night and subzero temperatures, bound for Nashville. I would set up a home office there to continue my work for Hal Leonard.

MAYBERRY, ANDY, AND ME

Let's go down to the fishin' hole!

And the best fishin' hole in the world was seen every week for eight seasons on CBS-TV in *The Andy Griffith Show*. The show's initial primetime run was from October 3, 1960, until April 1, 1968. But in the more than fifty years since its premiere, the show has never been off the air. Truly incredible. That easily puts it in the same league as *I Love Lucy* and a handful of other very successful TV shows from that era. Who would have thought that my path would eventually connect with that of *The Andy Griffith Show*'s titular actor?

I was at Quad Studios in Nashville producing a project. Quad is a popular studio right off the famed Music Row. Often when recording in a studio, where there are several rooms in which to record, musicians and producers bump into each other during our respective breaks from recording. Such was the case that day when I ran into my friend Dave Huntsinger, who was playing piano on another session there that day.

Dave Huntsinger is one of the most talented, intelligent, and funny people I've ever known. His razor-sharp wit is matched only by his musicianship. He's what is referred to in studio musician and producer circles as a "first call" player, meaning that whenever a call goes out for a recording session (in his case, for a pianist), he's the first one the producer or contractor calls. Therefore, first call players are the best players in town, and Dave has certainly proven that time and time again. He is also a very talented composer and arranger (among his credits is the legendary sacred children's musical published in the late 1970s, *Down by the Creek Bank*, which was a huge hit and is still being performed more than forty-five years after its initial release).

"What's happening, Mark?" asked Dave.

I told him about the project I was working on that day and then asked what he was working on.

"Andy Griffith singing hymns," he replied.

"You're kidding," I said. "Is Barney here too?"

Dave reported that Andy had decided he wanted to do a recording (titled *I Love to Tell the Story*) of his favorite hymns and enlisted famed entrepreneur-producer (now late) Billy Ray Hearn to assist and release it on his Sparrow Records label. (Billy Ray Hearn, as I continue to shamelessly name-drop, was another friend who could warrant an entire chapter in this book. Google his name and you can read all about his incredible and legendary career.)

I then asked the logical question that I ask in such cases: "Is there any music print planned on the project?" I knew this would be a perfect songbook for Hal Leonard to publish.

"No, not that I know of," said Dave.

"Well, we should change that!" I said.

Dave agreed that a matching print folio (as they're sometimes called) would be great. A print folio is simply a companion printed songbook that contains the same songs in music print as are found on the recording.

"I'll give Andy a call and see if he's interested. If he is, I'll let you know and set up a time for you to speak with him," Dave told me.

What a treat it would be to work with Andy Griffith, I thought. But I had no idea what to expect.

A few days later, I heard from Dave. Andy was indeed interested in a matching songbook for his project and was ready to speak with me. Dave and I set up a time for me to call Andy on the following day. My mind started thinking of the famed *Andy Griffith Show* and how Andy got his start in show business.

Andy Griffith was born in Mount Airy, North Carolina (Mount Airy became "Mayberry"). Griffith's early career was as a monologist, delivering long stories such as *What It Was, Was Football*, which is told from the point of view of a rural backwoodsman trying to figure out what was going on in a football game. The monologue was released as a single in 1953 and was a hit for Griffith, reaching number nine on the charts in 1954.

Griffith starred in Ira Levin's one-hour television version of *No Time for Sergeants* (March 1955) — a story about a country boy in the United States Air Force. He expanded that role in Ira Levin's full-length theatrical version of the same name on Broadway (October 1955). "Mr. Griffith does not have to condescend to Will Stockdale [his role in the play]," wrote Brooks Atkinson in *The New York Times*. "All he has to do is walk on the stage and look the audience straight in the face. If the armed forces cannot cope with Will Stockdale, neither can the audience resist Andy Griffith."

Griffith later reprised his role for the film version of *No Time for Sergeants* (1958); the film also featured Don Knotts as a corporal in charge of manual dexterity tests, marking the beginning of a lifelong association between Griffith and Knotts. *No Time for Sergeants* is considered the direct inspiration for the later television situation comedy *Gomer Pyle, U.S.M.C.*

Andy's only other New York stage appearance was the titular role in the 1957 musical *Destry Rides Again*, costarring Dolores Gray. The musical ran for 472 performances – lasting more than a year on Broadway.

In 1957, Griffith made his film debut starring in *A Face in the Crowd*. Although he played a country boy, this country boy was manipulative and power-hungry, a drifter who became a television host and used his show as a gateway to political power. He won critical praise for the role.

If his success on *The Andy Griffith Show* wasn't enough, lightning then struck a second time for him when he starred for nine seasons on TV's *Matlock*.

At last the time came for me to speak to Andy. I dialed the phone number provided by Dave, and lo and behold, Andy himself answered.

"Hi, Andy. This is Mark Cabaniss, and I'm calling to talk about possibly doing a songbook for your new CD."

"Sure, Mark. Dave told me you were going to call. So how do we make this book happen?"

His tone and speech rhythm weren't at all like Andy Taylor of Mayberry. Even though (as this book plainly proves!) I've met various celebrities over the years, it's hard to divorce yourself at first from their public personas. I was certainly expecting Andy Taylor to answer the phone that day, but Andy Griffith did instead. He was all business.

We discussed the details of what it would take to make the book happen. One idea I had was to make the book more of a souvenir fan book – meaning it would contain pictures and background information on Andy and *The Andy Griffith Show* and information on the songs contained in the book. Since all the musical material in the book was familiar hymns (easily found in hundreds of books already on the market), I knew that a great incentive for people to purchase this new songbook would be pictures and other background information on the beloved Andy Griffith that they could find only in this particular book. Andy agreed with and liked that approach. He sent me pictures from both *The Andy Griffith Show* and *Matlock*.

Over the next several weeks, we worked together on selecting the exact photos to be included in the book and reviewing the music manuscripts and text of the information to be included about him in the book. Once, when I received one of the first of Andy's many voice mails to me, I forwarded it to a friend at Hal Leonard whom I knew was a big fan of Andy. I heard later that day the voice mail had subsequently been forwarded all over Hal Leonard… to about a hundred employees or more. It was instant confirmation that even then, Andy still had a loyal fan base.

Andy was always very cooperative and responsive. As I got to know him better, he warmed up more and more. After we had been working together a few weeks, I finally got up enough courage to start asking him about some of his past projects, especially his signature Andy Griffith Show. Some actors who have been involved in hit shows shy away from discussing them in an effort not to dwell on past successes, but not Andy. He seemed delighted to discuss his old show.

"The *Griffith Show* was the best eight years of my life," he said. "But it wasn't an easy start," he added.

In 1960, Griffith appeared as a county sheriff (who was also a justice of the peace and the editor of the local newspaper) in an episode of *Make Room for Daddy*, starring Danny Thomas. This episode, in which Thomas's character was stopped for speeding in a little town, served as a backdoor pilot for *The Andy Griffith Show*. But the early script drafts of the first few episodes weren't right.

"They were making fun of southerners…making them come off like hicks," Andy said. He wanted the show not to have jokes per se, but for the comedy to arise from the characters being themselves and the often funny situations in which the characters would find themselves.

"I told [Executive Producer] Sheldon Leonard that I knew a couple of writers who would capture the style I knew it needed to have." Those writers were Jim Fritzell and Everett Greenbaum.

"We had great writers for the show during its run. Harvey Bullock was another who co-wrote dozens of episodes with Everett." Bullock and Greenbaum invented the idea of Barney having only one bullet in his gun, along with his signature catch phrase, "Nip it in the bud!"

The opening title sequence of Andy and son Opie walking leisurely down a dirt road with their fishing poles to a lake along with the inimitable whistling theme song looked as if it was filmed right in the heart of North Carolina. Actually, Andy explained, it was filmed in Los Angeles.

"We filmed the opening at a man-made reservoir in LA's Franklin Canyon just west of Coldwater Canyon," he said. For the last couple of decades, it's been parkland, open to the public for walking, hiking, and picnicking.

The opening theme was written (and whistled) by famed composer Earle Hagen (who also wrote music for other well-known shows such as *The Dick Van Dyke Show, Gomer Pyle, U.S.M.C., That Girl, Eight Is Enough*, and *The Mod Squad*).

"Earle is a fine musician and person," said Andy. "His music really set the tone for the show every week. I don't think anything as unique as that whistling theme song has ever been done before or since then."

Over the years, I'd heard the actress who played Aunt Bee (Frances Bavier) was not always easy to get along with. I wanted to find out if that was true, so I asked.

"Frances was hypersensitive. She got her feelings hurt easily, and that made her difficult to work with at times. But looking at the shows, you would never know that. She always did excellent work and never let her feelings get in the way of her work. But there were many times when we all felt like we were walking on eggshells around her."

To Bavier's credit, he said, several years after the series was over he got an unexpected phone call from her, by then retired and living in Siler City, North Carolina.

"Frances called and apologized for the way she sometimes acted during the show," he recalled. "We had a wonderful discussion and healed any old wounds." Not long after that phone call, Bavier died. Andy was thankful for the positive closure.

"Frances was with the show longer than any other cast member, and she really provided a special element," he said.

I then wanted to hear something from Andy that very few people might know about the show. Were there any particularly funny events and/or memories from making the show?

"I'll never forget when we filmed the episode when Barney deputizes several of the local citizens." In the scene, as only Don Knotts could do as Deputy Barney Fife, as he paced back and forth and "inspected the troops," he warned his new charges that there were two kinds of lawmen: "the quick and the dead."

Andy continued: "We had to shoot that scene about a dozen times because Hal Smith [Otis] and the rest of them kept cracking up, laughing at Don's brilliant performance."

We spoke of Ron Howard (Opie) as well.

"I'm very proud of Ronnie. He was always very observant on the set of the *Griffith Show* and was obviously learning a lot about the process of production." Of course, Ron Howard became one of Hollywood's most successful directors after a very successful career as an actor.

Why did he think the series lasted as long as it has with no signs of slowing down?

"Well, though we never said it, and though it was shot in the '60s, it had a feeling of the '30s. It was when we were doing it, of a time gone by."

Indeed, the ratings for the show were equally popular in major metropolitan areas and in rural towns, reflecting a nation's interest in a simpler time and place.

The series never placed lower than seventh in the Nielsen ratings and ended its final season at number one. It has been ranked by *TV Guide* as the ninth best show in American television history. The show spawned its own spin-off series, *Gomer Pyle, U.S.M.C.* (1964), a sequel series, *Mayberry R.F.D.* (1968), and a reunion television movie, *Return to Mayberry* (1986). The show's enduring popularity has also generated countless show-related merchandise.

We also discussed the series *Matlock*. Andy had concluded its run several years before our discussion.

"Dean Hargrove created *Matlock* and is one of the best writers I've ever known. They've talked about me doing specials and bringing back the show on a limited basis, but I really don't want to do that these days."

Although, numerically, Griffith appeared in more episodes portraying Sheriff Andy Taylor in *The Andy Griffith Show*, he logged more on-screen time as Ben Matlock due to the length of each show. As I got to know Andy better during our work together, I realized he was personally closer to being more like Ben Matlock than Andy Taylor.

"I wish I had more Andy Taylor in me," he said. "But that's not who I am."

Andy died on July 3, 2012. However, he'll live forever in reruns, and therefore will always be more than just "a face in the crowd."

THE UNSINKABLE MUSIC MAN

G MO^2H

Nope, that's not the chemical equation for a precious metal. It's my precious secret code that means "Get Me Out of Here." I use that shorthand whenever I feel the need to vacate a situation for whatever reason. Immediately.

It was intermission at the dress rehearsal of my hometown community theatre's production of the Broadway classic *The Music Man*. I was twenty-one years old, and although the summer before I had conducted a small pit orchestra in that same pit for a children's musical, this was a full, twenty-two-piece orchestra of paid professional musicians. And it was not going well.

GMO^2H

In my mind, I had three options:
1. Leave before act 2 began and drive to Europe. It would be tough crossing the Atlantic, but if my car stalled I could just swim.
2. Fake a heart attack from the podium, gain sympathy, and spend a week in the hospital.
3. Channel great conductor Leonard Bernstein and scare the living daylights out of all of the musicians into playing up a storm.

My thoughts raced as I walked back to the conductor's podium. *Why did I agree to do this? What was I thinking?* Regardless, I bravely gave the downbeat for the beginning music of act 2, and we were off. Little did I know this trial by fire was great preparation for the inevitable pressure-packed conducting situations that would follow in years to come.

Fortunately, there's a nice Hollywood ending to my Music Man story. On the opening night of the show, everything came together beautifully in the pit, and the production was a bona fide hit. I found out several years later that the original Broadway production of the show suffered some similar bumps in the road on its way to immortality. And I heard that (well, indirectly) from Meredith Willson himself. More on that later.

But first: "Words holler at me."

So wrote Meredith Willson in the opening to his book *But He Doesn't Know the Territory*. The book tells of *The Music Man* and its long, painful trek to Broadway. That trek to Broadway took seven long years, forty songs written (sixteen of which made it into the final show), and thirty versions of the script. (I hasten to add that most shows' treks to Broadway are painful.) And although he was a seasoned professional, Meredith was a novice regarding Broadway and, indeed, didn't "know the territory."

Words did "holler" at Meredith Willson. He said, "Words have a rhythm to them," and the sounds of life all around us are musical…such as a train, birds, bells, a clip-clopping horse, the ocean, or the word *love*. If we'll just stop and listen, we'll hear the "music" of life.

And Meredith Willson's career "hollered" at me.

Here was a man who pursued and blended his interests in composing, broadcasting, publishing, conducting, book writing, and playwriting into a phenomenally successful career (against substantial odds, I later found out). I have all the same (somewhat diverse) interests as he had. His success at pursuing all of them inspired (and inspires) me to do the same. Besides, Meredith was an instrumentalist and "band man" from way back, and that's right up my alley as well.

Another wonderful thing I found out about Meredith the more I researched him and spoke to those who knew him best was that he never allowed other people to define him in any way. *He defined himself.* I liked that. And I was determined to do the same.

That community theatre production I conducted of *The Music Man* introduced me to Meredith and sparked an interest to learn more about who this obviously talented man was.

Although the show is about a con man (Professor Harold Hill) who fleeces a small town and its citizens by using the ruse and promise of starting a boys' band (for which Hill is completely unqualified to do), I eventually came to realize the show is really about the transforming power of music.

I set out to find out all I could about Meredith Willson. That pursuit eventually led me to his front doorstep in Los Angeles.

Meredith was born in Mason City, Iowa, back in 1902. In addition to writing the book, music, and lyrics for *The Music Man*, he wrote the scores for two more Broadway musicals, *The Unsinkable Molly Brown* (1960) and *Here's Love* (1963).

Side note: As you read earlier, I got to know Fred Waring's widow, Virginia, quite well. Since I had read in one of Meredith's books that he and Fred Waring were friends, I asked Virginia if she had any good Meredith Willson stories. She smiled and said that she and Fred always enjoyed their visits with Meredith and his wife, Rini, and that they were gracious and entertaining hosts. She said one thing in particular she remembered was the time she and Fred joined Meredith and Rini for dinner in Hollywood. She noticed Meredith had a bandage on an index finger, and she asked what had happened.

"Oh, that's my writing hand," Meredith replied. "And I've been writing music and lyrics all week with my pencil in that hand, so I've developed a blister on that finger."

"Really?" said Virginia. "What are you writing?"

"A new musical," said Meredith.

"What's it called?" asked Virginia.

"My original title was 'The Silver Triangle,' but we just changed it to '*The Music Man*,'" replied Meredith.

Good call, Meredith. And the rest, as they say, is history.

Many of Meredith's individual songs became standards, performed by the likes of Glenn Miller, Frank Sinatra, Bing Crosby, Tommy Dorsey, Peggy Lee, and even The Beatles (they recorded an arrangement of his "Till There Was You" from *The Music Man*). Meredith's songs also showed up in movies and television series with or without credit. At the top of the list are "Trouble," "Till There Was You," "76 Trombones," and "It's Beginning to Look (a Lot) Like Christmas," followed by "The Wells Fargo Wagon," "Lida Rose," "I See the Moon," and "May the Good Lord Bless and Keep You."

The inhabitants of Mason City made a profound impression on Meredith – and many of them would later materialize in *The Music Man*.

He learned to play the flute and piccolo as a child, and in high school he got plenty of experience as a member of the marching band. He would live at home, however, only until the age of seventeen when, with a battered piccolo in his pocket, he took a train to New York City and enrolled in the Damrosch Institute of Musical Art (later to become the Juilliard School).

Shortly thereafter, Meredith joined the band of John Philip Sousa. With Sousa between 1921 and 1923, he toured the U.S., Cuba, and Mexico. From late 1924 to 1929 he was the principal flutist with the New York Chamber Music Society and the New York Philharmonic Orchestra under the legendary Arturo Toscanini.

During the 1930s Meredith was on the West Coast, first in San Francisco as concert director for radio station KFRC, then in Hollywood as a musical director for NBC Radio. Inevitably, as soon as the movie industry developed soundtracks he was writing music for films, usually uncredited. In 1940 he composed the score to Charlie Chaplin's film *The Great Dictator*, earning an Academy Award nomination for Best Original Score, and in 1941 arranging the music for *The Little Foxes* (starring Bette Davis), which snagged another nomination: Best Music Scoring of a Dramatic Picture.

World War II intervened, during which Willson served as a major in the U.S. Armed Forces Radio Service. He performed as a bandleader on *The Burns and Allen Show*, sometimes taking part as a regular comic character. This show continued for some time after the war while Willson returned to directing the music for various radio and television networks.

Another offshoot of Armed Forces Radio Service programming was *The Big Show*, a Sunday night NBC radio variety showcase hosted by Tallulah Bankhead that ran for two seasons (1950–51). Meredith, as music director and interlocutor (his running gags always began, "Well, sir, Miss Bankhead...."), wrote the song that closed each installment, "May the Good Lord Bless and Keep You." He also worked with Jack Benny's show on CBS and was a regular panelist on the game show *The Name's the Same*.

So how did a man with this particular background come to write a hit Broadway show? I kept digging to find out.

In 1950, while working at the Hollywood Bowl, Willson met writer Franklin Lacey, who would later help him develop the story line for the musical that would become *The Music Man*. This "Iowan's attempt to pay tribute to his home state," (as he called it) starring Robert Preston and Barbara Cook, opened on Broadway in December 1957, won six Tony Awards including Best Musical, and ran for a hefty 1,375 performances until April 1961. Its Original Cast Album won the first Grammy Award ever offered in its category.

The Music Man was then adapted for the screen twice: first in 1962 as a major Warner Brothers motion picture starring Robert Preston (who reprised his Broadway role as Harold Hill) along with Shirley Jones and then in 2003 for ABC-TV starring Matthew Broderick.

The stage version enjoyed two Broadway revivals: first at City Center with Dick Van Dyke in 1980 and twenty years later – long after Meredith's death – at the Neil Simon Theatre, earning eight Tony nominations and eight Drama Desk nominations and running for 699 performances. I was fortunate to see this production of the show on Broadway, and I can say firsthand it was spectacular. I'm sure Meredith would have been pleased (but then, I believe he was probably aware of it and hovering over it somehow!).

Meredith's musical accomplishments were not limited to musical theatre; he wrote classical music in many genres: two symphonies, orchestral suites, symphonic poems, chamber music, and a grand secular oratorio for orchestra, choir, and vocal soloist. He also composed hymns and anthems for his church.

Fast-forward to my first job. I was at Kentucky Wesleyan College managing radio station WKWC-FM, and there was a weekly show on the station that focused on pop and Broadway music. Why not do a half-hour show devoted to Meredith and his musicals?

I researched and researched (this was before the days of the Internet) and wrote the script. But I really wanted to interview someone who knew Meredith and could speak with authority on his life and career. Meredith had died in 1984…and by then it was 1988. Although my initial interest in him had started several years earlier when I first conducted *The Music Man*, it wasn't until I had the platform of WKWC that I could put my interest into action. And Meredith's obituary mentioned that he was survived by his wife, Rosemary (Rini had died from cancer in 1966).

As a newly minted member of ASCAP (the American Society of Composers, Authors and Publishers), I reached out to my ASCAP contact in New York City to see if she might know how to contact Mrs. Willson. I knew Meredith had been a long-time ASCAP member, and…well, my aforementioned mantra kicked in: Nothing ventured, nothing gained!

Indeed, ASCAP agreed to call Rosemary and see if she was open to me interviewing her for the program. Mrs. Willson said, "Yes" (!), and ASCAP gave me her phone number.

I called Mrs. Willson for the interview, and we seemed to hit it off. After all, I was one of her late husband's biggest fans, and she picked up on that quickly. I asked her what she thought helped Meredith succeed at so many ventures.

"Meredith always said if you're really interested in something and pursue it passionately and happen to be in the right place at the right time, your chances of success are improved. He said one thing can lead to another.

"That was certainly the case in Meredith's career. When he went to New York right out of high school and got the job with Sousa and eventually joined the New York Philharmonic, that led to his being invited to audition for the orchestra in Seattle. That didn't pan out but instead led to him being offered a job in radio in San Francisco, which eventually led to a job at NBC radio.

"All the while he was conducting orchestras on radio he was also writing music. That was great experience for him."

So I popped my burning question. Just how did he come to write a musical comedy?

"It was while he was involved with Armed Forces Radio that he met Frank Loesser [composer of the hit musical *Guys and Dolls*]. Frank encouraged Meredith to write a musical comedy based on the many stories he told on radio about his hometown in Iowa, Mason City," she said.

"Meredith always said he started writing *The Music Man* just to prove to Frank and others that he couldn't do it," Rosemary said. "But looks like he was very wrong," she added with a laugh.

What was one of his secrets to success, if he had one? I asked.

"He loved people. He loved his career as a musician and an author and embraced life. He was so at ease with everyone and made everyone feel right at home. He was a loving person…not only in public but at home as well. He treated everyone the same…with respect…from United States presidents to cab drivers."

My interview with Mrs. Willson was drawing to a close, but being me, I couldn't resist pressing my luck just a bit.

"If I come to Los Angeles in the future, would it be okay if I stopped by to say hello?" I cautiously asked.

"Absolutely," she replied.

Of course, I was elated. Mrs. Willson might have thought it was a long shot that some kid living in Kentucky would ever get to Los Angeles, but she was cordial, nevertheless.

Well, naturally, when a trip developed for me to go to Los Angeles later that year, I gave her a call in advance to see if I could drop by. She was happy to visit with me in her and Meredith's home in Los Angeles (actually Brentwood, California – an LA suburb).

Mrs. Willson greeted me at the door and ushered me into her spacious living room, where a lot of memorabilia was placed. There was a miniature version of the fictional River City, Iowa (where *The Music Man* takes place); hanging on one wall were pictures of Meredith with several U.S. presidents; other walls had pictures of him with various celebrities such as Frank Sinatra and George Burns. And in the midst of it all were two interlocking grand pianos.

Pointing to one of them, Rosemary said, "This is the piano on which Meredith did all of his composing, including *The Music Man*."

I then noticed a large photo of what looked like a parade with a marching band.

"What was this all about?" I asked.

"That is quite a story," she said as a big smile crossed her face. "Meredith was good friends with Walt Disney. Walt had a special dining room which overlooked Main Street at his Disneyland Theme Park. One night, he had Meredith and Rini for dinner at that private dining room.

"After dinner, before dessert was served, Walt politely excused himself and then returned carrying what looked like a marching band drum major's coat. He asked Meredith to put it on. Meredith did and it fit like a glove. Walt then went to a drawer and pulled out a conductor's baton and gave it to Meredith. He then motioned for Meredith and Rini to go to the veranda, where French doors opened onto a balcony overlooking Main Street at Disneyland.

"At the precise moment when Meredith opened the French doors, Walt blew a drum major's whistle, and a marching band started coming down Main Street. The band was filled completely with trombones…776 of them to be exact…and Meredith then conducted his own '76 Trombones' (from *The Music Man*) from that balcony. This photo is the fold-out picture that was in *Life* magazine of that trombone band."

We sat and visited for an hour, speaking about Meredith and his work. As we were coming to the end of our visit, I shared my most important thought with her about her late husband's greatest achievement.

"I think what Meredith was trying to say with *The Music Man* is not that seeing is believing, but that *believing is seeing*."

"I think I know what you mean," she said, her curiosity piqued.

I continued, "Early in the musical, no one could see the band that Professor Harold Hill was supposedly assembling – because there wasn't one. But when the citizens of River City believed there was a band and 'saw' that band, their lives were transformed. They had to 'believe' before they could 'see' it. That's faith.

"Nothing had actually changed in River City, other than their belief that things could be better. And for one thing, that meant they started to treat each other with more respect and kindness. Suddenly, as they forgot their differences and 'Iowa stubborn' ways, they had hope and faith in something bigger than themselves. The transforming power of music had triumphed."

Mrs. Willson was grinning like Winthrop with his new cornet (and if you don't get that analogy, go see the show!).

"That's it. Meredith always believed in the power of music and its ability to change lives," she said.

I then mentioned the picture on the wall of Meredith with Frank Sinatra.

"Meredith and Frank were friends, but there was the time that Meredith had to put his foot down about something concerning Frank."

"Oh, really? Do tell." This had to be a good story.

"After *The Music Man* had been such a hit on Broadway and Warner Brothers had bought the film rights, Jack Warner told Meredith that he didn't want Robert Preston [who had originated the lead role of Harold Hill on Broadway] to do the part in the film. He wanted Frank Sinatra to do it," she explained.

"But Meredith was a man of his convictions and knew that no one could do the role better than Bob Preston. Meredith called Jack and said if Bob didn't do the film, he wouldn't allow it to be made."

Of course, Robert Preston did the role in the film, and thanks to Meredith, his immortal performance is preserved on film.

I couldn't resist telling her about me conducting a production of *The Music Man* in my hometown. The richness of telling the story only a few feet away from the very piano on which he wrote that show wasn't lost on me in that moment.

"We had a rough dress rehearsal. But the show was a hit," I told her.

"Meredith had some tough times with that show, especially during the Philadelphia tryout. Some songs had to be rewritten and moved around, and there were terrible sound problems. But they got everything ironed out for the Broadway opening," she said, pointing to the framed *Playbill* of the original production hanging on the wall.

We soon concluded our time together, and I bid her good-bye with a hug. I had reached my goal of connecting at the highest possible level with the person who would have known Meredith best, and it was a delightful visit. She also connected me with her estate attorney at the historic entertainment law firm of Gang, Tyre, Raymer and Brown in Beverly Hills – for any future ideas I might have on how to continue to perpetuate Meredith's legacy. Rosemary and I exchanged Christmas cards for several years afterward, until she passed away.

Meredith Willson's legacy is solidly preserved first and foremost through *The Music Man*, but also through The Music Man Square, the aforementioned multimillion-dollar foundation and museum located in Mason City.

About a decade after my visit with Rosemary Willson, I received a call from a music retailer friend who was located in Kansas City. He said he had tossed my name in the hat to be the featured clinician at the annual Iowa

Choral Directors Convention. That year's convention was going to take place in Mason City.

A few weeks later, my phone rang. It was a representative from the Iowa Choral Directors Association calling, asking if I would like to be one of their featured clinicians at their annual convention.

I said, "Yes," faster than Robert Preston could perform "Trouble in River City."

My three days in Mason City were incredible. The people were wonderful. I met Carl Miller who was then the Executive Director of The Music Man Square (www.themusicmansquare.org). Carl and I hit it off so well, he installed me on the Board of Advisors for the organization. I also visited Meredith's restored boyhood home and saw the room where he was born, among other famous spots from his childhood, such as his home church, the First Congregational United Church of Christ.

As I noted earlier, one of Meredith's most famous songs (that everyone sang at the end of *The Big Show* radio program) was "May the Good Lord Bless and Keep You." Meredith was inspired to write this song because his mother taught a children's Sunday school class at the First Congregational United Church of Christ. At the end of each class, as the children left the room, Rosalie Willson would say to each child, "May the good Lord bless and keep you." One of the concerts I conducted during my stay in Mason City was at that church. The choir sang several of my published anthems, but I got to select a few additional pieces, and naturally, I selected a choral arrangement of "May the Good Lord Bless and Keep You." I conducted it at the end of the concert from the balcony of the church. I felt the strong presence of Meredith (and his mother, Rosalie) hovering through the room. I stopped by Rosalie's old Sunday school classroom after the concert that night. As I stood there in that quiet room, I said softly to Meredith and Rosalie, "May the good Lord bless and keep you."

When Meredith moved to California, he remained active in the United Church of Christ as a member and deacon of Westwood Hills Congregational Church in Los Angeles. He donated a stained glass window, known as *"The*

Music Man Window," above the pew where he sat, which represented various musical instruments. The window still glows there.

Another bonus was that years later, The Music Man Square placed into their archives the radio show about Meredith I had produced and narrated (featuring the interview with Rosemary Willson).

Meredith Willson died of heart failure at the age of eighty-two, and he is buried in Mason City. I visited the cemetery during my Mason City trip and paid my respects to him. Rosemary Willson died in 2010 at the age of eighty-eight after a lengthy illness.

Even after Meredith's death, the accolades and awards kept coming to him, including the Presidential Medal of Freedom, awarded to him posthumously in 1987 by President Ronald Reagan. In 1999, the United States Postal Service issued a postage stamp featuring Meredith (I have a first issue copy of the stamp framed and hanging in my office, "hovering over the proceedings"). Also, Meredith's estate continues to support The Music Man Square and numerous other charities and music-related causes. And in 2005, Rosemary Willson donated several million dollars to fund the construction of a new (and the only) residence hall at Meredith's alma mater, The Juilliard School of Music in New York City. River City is the gift that keeps on giving.

I'm so glad I conducted that second act of *The Music Man* that fateful night and didn't drive to Europe. That night was evidently Meredith's first lesson in teaching me how to become "unsinkable."

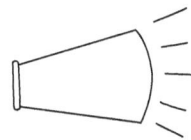

WAIT, WAIT... THERE'S MORE!

Meredith's funny, engaging book *But He Doesn't Know the Territory* is back in print and as of this writing available through Amazon.com. Even if you're not a musical theatre fan, I encourage you to read it if you enjoy hilarious and inspiring accounts of overcoming substantial obstacles.

GOOD-BYE, UNCLE HAL

After ten years, I had gotten to know "Uncle Hal" (Leonard, that is) very well. Uncle Hal was dependable, successful, and solid, even if "he" was at times a bit quirky and set in his ways. But then, so am I.

My time at Hal Leonard had been very good. We had grown (practically from scratch) their church music division to a multimillion-dollar enterprise. In addition to expanding their sacred choral line of products, I had beaten the bushes to sign print deals with several Christian music publishers for Hal Leonard to become their print music publisher for various songbooks. I was very proud of our successes.

And I clung to an earlier discussion that Larry Morton and I had prior to my move back to Nashville of me continuing to grow the church side of the company by adding a telesales person or persons in Nashville, an assistant, and perhaps an on-site editor instead of having all those functions located in the Milwaukee headquarters. On several occasions, church music activities had been pushed to the side in Milwaukee due to other pressing areas needing attention. I certainly understood that, but without me on the ground in Milwaukee anymore, I felt that having a small staff who got out of bed every day to focus 100 percent on Hal Leonard church music would fuel further growth. Several in upper management agreed and said they felt sure the day would come and that would happen.

But it never did. Year after year. Four years to be exact after moving back to Nashville. And I was starting to get restless. Again.

If that weren't enough, the typical music business strange bedfellow pairings had continued, this time with a company near and dear to me. Zomba (Brentwood Music's owner by then, you'll remember) sold to BMG, a global German-based music publishing and record company. BMG's print deal was with Hal Leonard, so suddenly, all the Brentwood Music print sales force (now called Brentwood-Benson because of Brentwood's acquisition of the Benson Music Company) became Hal Leonard employees. My worlds were colliding and getting smaller. It was discussed that I might have a larger role in addition to my duties at Hal Leonard, helping assimilate and manage the Brentwood-Benson employees who had become Hal Leonard employees, but that was never to be.

With the realization that I was probably going to be a one-man band stuck in a home office all by myself for the foreseeable future, even with Hal Leonard now having a larger presence in Nashville due to its addition of the Brentwood-Benson employees, I felt at a crossroads in my career. I walked up to the second floor in my house and gazed out of a window over the trees and past the nearby foothills.

For some reason, whenever I have a major decision to make in my life, if I can see the horizon, sunrise, sunset, mountains, or beach, it gives me clarity. I feel as if I see God particularly in those places, sense His presence, and listen to His voice. In that moment, I realized I needed to call Barrie Edwards and see what was happening these days with Shawnee Press. I knew that Lynn Sengstack, Shawnee's VP/CEO, had left about a year before, and I had heard things were a bit adrift at Shawnee of late.

After an eight-year tenure at Shawnee Press, Lynn had left to be a part of her family's music publishing business. She later told me she left because she "saw the handwriting on the wall" as Music Sales continued to absorb Shawnee's operations into theirs, creating less independence for

Shawnee. I was feeling the itch to start my own company or otherwise do something to move my career forward, which now seemed to be stalled. Perhaps there was some sort of joint venture I could do with Music Sales wherein I could start my own company and they would partner with me, while I could offer some guidance and input to the now leaderless Shawnee Press.

Barrie and I had run into each other at industry events a few times over the years since my visit with him in New York City several years back, and our meetings had always been cordial. So the next day, I picked up the phone, took a deep breath, and called Barrie. It had been a few years since I had seen him. I hoped he would remember me positively. He took the call and was immediately welcoming.

"Hello, Mahk," he said in that wonderful accent. "How have you been?" We caught up, and he said he had been continuing to watch my career, especially since I had made the move to Hal Leonard back in 1995. I told him that while I had enjoyed my time at Hal, I was contemplating making a move to start my own company. He was very interested in hearing more, so I told him a few ideas on how we might work together. He was so interested in the ideas, he suggested I come to New York to discuss it with him.

So a decade after my first meeting with Barrie, I found myself once again stepping off an airplane at New York's La Guardia airport to meet with him. It was December, so the weather was cold and blustery. But I didn't care because I was excited about the meeting.

This time with Barrie was different from that first one years earlier. I had now gleaned an additional ten years of experience in the music business in my time with Hal Leonard, and those years were valuable for me. Barrie was enthusiastic speaking with me, and after about an hour of catching up and discussing business, he offered to take me out to lunch. We went to a nearby restaurant on Park Avenue. It was there he "popped the question."

As I spoke to him about how we could possibly partner on a joint venture, I could almost see the wheels turning in his head. After he finished his entrée, he said eight glorious words to me: "What would you think about running Shawnee Press?"

Those words would alter the course of my life (and several others) forever. The thought had obviously crossed my mind since my reconnection with him, especially since Lynn Sengstack was no longer there. From the outside, it seemed to be plugging along led by an internal management team. Not the case, according to Barrie.

"Shawnee is not performing as well as we would like it to," said Barrie. He added there had been some internal management team conflicts, and since the 9/11 attacks in 2001, sales had slipped and were continuing to gradually shrink.

All my memories of Shawnee came rushing back. I was excited about the idea of being in charge of this publisher I had connected with many years ago. I didn't have to think about it.

I said, "Yes," faster than Fred Waring could whip up a milkshake (or adult beverage) in his Waring blender.

Barrie said, "Let's speak more about this next week. I would like to tell Bob about our discussion, and I'll be in touch." Barrie and I shook hands, and I was soon on my way back home to Nashville.

Bob was the aforementioned Bob Wise, owner of Music Sales Corporation. As I learned about him, I found out that he was not without controversy and his detractors (as well as some supporters, of course). Such is usually the case with a high-profile figure like Bob Wise.

As promised, Barrie called the following week and told me he'd spoken with Bob about the idea of me running Shawnee Press. He said Bob would be coming to New York from London the next month and would like to meet with me. I needed to book a flight to New York, and they would make hotel and transportation accommodations for me. I looked forward to the meeting.

The Christmas season came as usual that year, but in the back of my mind during the gift giving, parties, and usual festivities was Shawnee Press. The meeting with Bob and Barrie was set for January 12. A few days before that, however, I had quite a scare.

I couldn't stop thinking about the upcoming meeting. As I lay in bed trying to doze off, my heart started fluttering, then skipping beats. Like everyone, I had experienced the occasional heart flutter or skipped beat. But this was different. It just wouldn't stop, and I couldn't quite catch my breath. This went on for about thirty minutes, and I decided it wasn't going to get any better…maybe it would get worse. Was I having a heart attack? Is this what it felt like? My heart was starting to beat faster and faster. I knew I had to get to the hospital.

At the emergency room, they took me immediately and hooked me up to various machines. My heart was still freaking out, and I told the nurse that they needed to give me some sort of sedative to calm me down. She injected me with something, and in a matter of seconds, it was as if someone was turning a knob on my emotions from "high" to "low." I was now calmer and chatting with the nurse about different things. My heart finally got back into rhythm thanks to some other injections, and they kept me overnight.

The next morning, the cardiologist explained I'd had a classic "afib" (atrial fibrillation) event, most likely brought on by stress. It was easy for me to figure out the stress involved the anticipation of the very important meeting that was happening the following week in New York. I guess something had to give, and it did. But perhaps now that was out of the way and I could focus on trying to relax and have a good meeting that could lead to me getting the keys to Shawnee Press.

The following Wednesday, I had an early flight out of Nashville to New York City. The plane left at 6:30 so I was up around 4:15. I always dread early morning flights, but when I woke up that day, I was enthusiastic and felt a real peace about the upcoming meeting that would happen later that morning in Manhattan. I was confident and excited.

Everything went like clockwork…the flight from Nashville to New York was on time and smooth. Barrie had arranged for a limo to pick me up at La Guardia, which was also right on time. I got to the Music Sales offices twenty minutes prior to my meeting and went to a corner coffee shop across the street to collect my thoughts. When the meeting time drew closer, I entered the skyscraper where Music Sales was located and pushed the same button on the elevator I'd pushed a decade before to transport me to the twentieth floor, and I was on my way.

I stepped out and saw the same grand piano in the Music Sales lobby that had been there forever. It was a legendary piano once owned by a famous twentieth-century composer…I think John Cage. The receptionist greeted me and told Barrie I was there. Barrie soon emerged with his usual affable manner intact, smiling and warm. "Hello, Mahk…welcome," he said, in that now familiar brogue. "Let's go meet Bob."

Now, once again, I was in the conference room where I had met with Barrie a decade earlier. "Déjà vu all over again" to quote Yogi Berra.

Bob Wise isn't a very tall man, bordering on short. He dresses impeccably, his movements are slow and deliberate, and his speech is measured. His eyes bulge a bit out of his head, and he has thinning white hair. All of these characteristics made him a fascinating physical study. He had a somewhat warm manner about him, even though I could tell he was very much sizing me up from the moment he met me. Although he had lived in London for years, he was originally from the United States and had no discernible accent.

Here was a very successful independent music publisher, known far and wide in the music publishing industry. Bob's company held European print rights to several major acts, including Bob Dylan, Jimi Hendrix, Eric Clapton, U2, AC/DC, Coldplay, Oasis, and ABBA. Bob was a man who had succeeded on his own terms. Years earlier, he had acquired the legendary G. Schirmer classical music catalog and was justifiably proud of that acquisition. The Schirmer offices were housed with the Music Sales offices on that same floor.

After briefly exchanging the usual pleasantries, Bob got down to business. He talked as if he had already made up his mind to hire me (based on Barrie's recommendation, I suppose), and we were hashing out the details of my employment. Once those were settled, he spoke a lot about what he wanted to see happen with Shawnee Press. He mentioned several things, but the main point he stressed was that he wanted it to grow once again. Period.

"Whatever it takes to make Shawnee grow again, Mark, I want you to do that," he said. I literally was taking notes and underlined that one twice.

One big point of discussion was whether or not to move Shawnee from its long-time Pennsylvania home to Nashville. Although Bob talked about the virtues of keeping it in Pennsylvania, he also liked the idea of Music Sales (by way of Shawnee Press) having a Nashville presence. Music Sales had offices in different parts of the world (including New York and Los Angeles), so a Nashville office made sense, since Nashville is a major music center (albeit primarily country and Christian music). Bob saw Shawnee as a primarily sacred publisher at this point (and justifiably so given its lesser market share in the school area by now) so being close to the Nashville Christian music scene made sense to him.

The meeting with Bob and Barrie lasted about ninety minutes, and then we went out to lunch in the neighborhood. We parted with warm handshakes, and Barrie said he would be in touch to wrap things up and get an employment contract to me.

An employment contract! It looked as if I was indeed going to get the keys to Shawnee Press! I was so filled with energy and enthusiasm, I didn't take a cab from 20th and Park Avenue all the way back to my hotel at 49th and Broadway but chose to walk. And as I walked, all those memories of the music of Shawnee Press, Fred Waring, Ruth Sibley, and on and on flashed before me.

Within a week, I had a contract from Barrie. All the final details were worked out. One major detail was that I would live in Pennsylvania for two to three months in a hotel while I transitioned Shawnee from Pennsylvania to Nashville. I signed the contract, and that was that. I was now officially the president of Shawnee Press. And they had agreed to move it to Nashville. I turned in my letter of resignation to Hal Leonard. They were surprised, but gracious (especially Larry Morton). We parted friends and remain so to this day.

During Shawnee's three-month transition from Pennsylvania to Nashville, I resided at the Shawnee Inn, located in Shawnee on Delaware, Pennsylvania. This historic hotel had once been owned by Fred Waring. Pictures of celebrities from Waring's heyday lined the halls: Jack Benny, George Burns, Jackie Gleason, and others. They had all played in Waring's famous golf tournaments at the Shawnee Inn in those days. The Inn was now a bit like an aging actress trying to hold on to her dignity. You knew that great things had once happened there, but the best days were behind her…somewhat like Shawnee Press, I was starting to realize. But I still had high hopes mixed with boundless energy and enthusiasm about the future.

During that transitional period, I was back and forth between Nashville and Pennsylvania several times, looking for office space and hiring the new staff (I personally reviewed more than three hundred resumes for the eight positions I needed to fill). I eventually settled on an office on Music Row. Barrie really liked the idea of having Shawnee located on Music Row. That office building is now often seen in the ABC-TV television series *Nashville* – interiors and exterior. It's bizarre seeing your old offices on primetime television.

If you've never been to Music Row in Nashville, it's an interesting two (long) streets filled with memories and significance. Music Square East and Music Square West run concurrently creating Music Row, which is populated by music publishers, record labels, studios, artist management firms, etc. Most of the offices on the streets are old refurbished homes, giving the area a real homey feel. Of course, there are several modern, impressive buildings: ASCAP, BMI, SESAC, Sony, CMT (Country Music Television), and others. The melding of the two architectural styles makes for an eclectic and interesting visual. Probably the most visited spot on Music Row is RCA's famous Studio B, where Elvis Presley and other famous artists of that era recorded.

So in the fall of 2005, I was fully settled with the new Shawnee Press staff in Nashville on Music Row. We moved all the archives and files, which was quite a job. The carefully chosen new staff was all in place, and we were united in our desire to make things happen. Bob Wise's words from our first meeting resonated in the back of my mind:

"Whatever it takes to make Shawnee grow again, Mark, I want you to do that."

The following four years and several months that followed were full of the usual and sometimes unusual challenges of running a music publisher. But it was an exciting and rewarding period for me.

Best of all, the new Shawnee team and I together accomplished the edict that Bob Wise had given me from the start: "Make Shawnee grow again." It did, and Virginia Waring herself noticed the new energy that was present with the company and mentioned it to me on several occasions. I even founded "The Fred Waring Choral Award" (through *The Instrumentalist* magazine), which Virginia greatly appreciated. High school choral directors coast to coast now present it annually to deserving choral students.

I will always be proud and thankful that I and the team I assembled were able to accomplish some good things for the Waring legacy and revive Shawnee Press for a period of time. I say for "a period of time" because unbeknownst to me, the winds of change were starting to blow again, but I would not feel those winds until more than four years into my tenure there.

HERE ON *GILLIGAN'S ISLAND* WITH *THE BRADY BUNCH*

So what do two iconic television series from the 1960s – *Gilligan's Island* and *The Brady Bunch* – have in common? Certainly not their characters or setting.

Both series were created by a person who became a television icon: Sherwood Schwartz.

Like many people my age, in the 1970s I loved to watch reruns of *Gilligan's Island* with an after-school snack (PB&J with chocolate milk). To adults, it was probably just a silly show (it was certainly seen that way by TV critics when it first premiered, although forty years later, some of them were more generous), but to kids, it was hilarious and a staple in our television viewing diet. And I think, truth be told, a lot of adults my age still remember the show fondly as a part of their childhood.

Fast-forward to years and years later...when I found myself standing on the edge of the *Gilligan's Island* lagoon! No Skipper or Gilligan...or Ginger or Mary Ann...or any of the other castaways were there. As a matter of fact, there was no water in the lagoon anymore. It had been converted into a parking lot! And the street running beside it was now named *"Gilligan's Island* Road."

Believe me, it's a long way from age nine and PB&J in North Carolina to the *Gilligan's Island* lagoon. Just how did I get there? ("There" was actually the CBS Studio Center back lot in Hollywood – Studio City, California, to be precise.)

After I produced a Steve Allen special for National Public Radio (more on that later), my contact at NPR asked me if I had ideas for additional shows. I was delighted that he wanted me to pitch more concepts, so I put on my thinking cap.

Since I had an affinity for television shows from the 1960s and 1970s, I wondered whether something might be there. Perhaps I could somehow parlay that interest into a special for NPR. The first idea I came up with was to interview some of the actors and creators of shows from that era and call the special "Those Were the Days." It might be fun for audiences to hear what Henry Winkler (The Fonz) now thinks of *Happy Days* or how Sherwood Schwartz came up with the ideas for *Gilligan's Island* and The Brady Bunch.

Hey! Now there's an idea, I thought. I was immediately excited about the prospect of reaching Sherwood Schwartz, who always seemed like a nice man when I'd seen him on television. So I called a Hollywood television friend and got Sherwood's contact info. My friend didn't have an e-mail address for him, only a mailing address. So I sent Mr. Schwartz a letter telling him about my idea and that I would like to visit with him for a possible radio show. I received a reply in a few weeks. It was a cordial letter in which he told me he would be happy for me to come and spend some time with him.

My flight was soon booked, and I was winging my way to LA. Sherwood Schwartz and *Gilligan's Island* awaited. I planned other business meetings to make the most out of my trek to the West Coast, but I was most excited about my meeting with Mr. Schwartz.

Although the CBS Corporation is headquartered in New York City (and its famed CBS Broadcast Center is located on Fifty-Seventh Street), its major television production facilities are in Los Angeles: Television City and Studio

Center. Television City is where many audience-type shows are produced (*The Price Is Right*, other game shows, some soap operas, etc.). Studio Center is where a multitude of CBS and other network shows have been produced over the years (*Seinfeld, Gunsmoke, The Wild, Wild West, CSI, Newhart,* etc.). It consists of several huge indoor soundstages and outdoor backlot sets. It was at CBS Studio Center where *Gilligan's Island* was filmed.

After landing in Los Angeles and picking up a rental car, I checked into my hotel in Studio City. Mr. Schwartz had asked me to meet him at the CBS Studio Center Commissary (a no-frills restaurant on the lot) for lunch.

At the studio gate on Radford Avenue, the guard checked me in and gave me directions to the commissary. After parking the car, I walked down a street where westerns were shot once upon a time. After taking a few more steps and turning a corner, I was suddenly walking down the street where outdoor scenes for *Seinfeld* were filmed. I soon came to the commissary. Standing out front was the gentle and smiling Sherwood Schwartz. He had surmised that I was the eager beaver approaching him.

"Hi, Mr. Schwartz!" I greeted him cheerfully.

"Hi, Mark. I knew it was you immediately," he responded. "And you can call me Sherwood."

We headed into the commissary and found a quiet corner. After the opening pleasantries and ordering, I was eager to talk about his illustrious career in television writing and producing. And what a career it had been. I turned on my little hand-held tape recorder and began by asking, "So how did you get into show business?"

Sherwood said his entertainment career came "by accident." He relocated from New York to Southern California to pursue a Master of Science degree in biology. In need of employment, he began writing jokes for Bob Hope's radio program, for which his brother, Al Schwartz, worked.

"Bob liked my jokes, used them on his show, and got big laughs. Then he asked me to join his writing staff. I was faced with a major decision—writing comedy or starving to death while I cured those diseases. I made a quick career change."

He went on to write for Ozzie Nelson's *The Adventures of Ozzie and Harriet* and other radio shows. He was also a writer for the Armed Forces Radio Network before he got his break in television, which included writing for *The Red Skelton Show*.

But where, I asked, did the idea for *Gilligan's Island* come from?

"Perhaps from my public speaking class at New York University, where I received my bachelor's degree," he said.

"What happened in that class that helped birth those seven castaways?" I asked.

"Well, Professor Borden was the instructor, and very often he would give us an exercise in making an impromptu speech. He would provide a topic; each student would then get up as called on and speak on that topic for one minute without any preparation.

"One day the topic was, 'If you were alone on a desert island what one thing would you like to have?'

"Two things were excluded by Professor Borden. One, any means of escape. And two, a woman. It was an all-male class! Several students said different things, but the one that stuck with me the most was that one person said 'a radio.' If the stranded person had a radio, he could learn what was going on in the outside world…all the news of the day."

He continued, "Truthfully, I don't honestly know where the ultimate concept for the show came from. But that discussion in class did stick with me. I also can't deny the possible influence of *Robinson Crusoe*. It was one of my favorite books when I was a kid. And besides, who hasn't thought at one time what it would be like to be stranded on a desert island?

"After leaving the *Skelton Show*, I worked on many ideas for TV series. Mostly comedy because that's how the networks perceive me – as a comedy person. I spent weeks going from one concept to another, looking for a fresh idea. Not another domestic sitcom or a bumbling private eye or a western spoof. I wanted something unique, a concept which I could say something important, even though it would be in comedic terms.

"One day the idea of a group of diverse characters being forced to live together began to take shape. They would be a 'family' but of a very different sort. But what brings them together? And why are they forced to stay together? Maybe a desert island, so there's little likelihood they would be found. And if their boat were wrecked, they couldn't escape."

As the idea continued to develop in his mind, he saw the possibility of social implications for the show underneath the comedy.

"A great many comic possibilities came to mind immediately, based on two major themes: the problems of modern man dealing with primitive life on an uninhabited island, and the conflicts among people as they are forced to adjust to each other. The world, in a real sense, is an island, where Americans and other nations and races and religions must somehow learn to live together on this 'island' we call Earth.

"I began to see that the characters stranded on this island could represent a social microcosm. They could represent extremes in social, intellectual, and financial terms, as well as in background, personality, and even size."

As a nine-year old, I simply saw it as a bunch of funny people trying to get off the island! But that's part of the magic of the series. While I believe it did end up appealing largely to children, it certainly had appealing elements for adults. True family viewing.

"No one ever got shot on *Gilligan's Island*, and we never saw any blood. But there were certainly threatening circumstances to add suspense," he said.

So where in the world did he come up with the name Gilligan?

"I knew I wanted the word *island* in the title, and I wanted the island to be named after the Skipper's hapless mate. Believe it or not, it took me three weeks to settle on the name Gilligan. It was important to me to have the right name.

"There are many names that would make the series sound like a dramatic show: *Johnson's Island*, *Thompson's Island*, *Wilson's Island*, and so forth. I also didn't want a ridiculous name like *Winkelpleck's Island* or *Hogfighter's Island*.

"So I just kept looking through phone book after phone book until I hit the name Gilligan. I felt Gilligan was funny enough to indicate a comedy series and acceptable enough to avoid burlesque."

I wanted to know some little secret about shooting the show and a little something about each cast member.

"We couldn't shoot any scenes in the lagoon during rush hour since the Hollywood Freeway was right behind the palm trees! You could hear the cars and trucks otherwise over the dialog.

"Bob [Denver – who played Gilligan] couldn't stand doing scenes in the lagoon, and he got thrown into that water a lot. He said it was nasty. And I decided he had a point when he told me he found a dead fish floating in it. So I had it drained, cleaned up, and refilled. He was happier about it after that.

"Bob was great to work with. He was actually quite a shy person, but when he got in front of the camera, he knew what to do. Alan [the Skipper] Hale was like a big teddy bear. Even when he got mad at Gilligan, you knew he still loved him. Had it been any other way, the audience wouldn't have liked the Skipper. I think the comedic chemistry between Bob and Alan was right up there with other great comedy duos, like Laurel and Hardy or Martin and Lewis.

"Russ [the Professor] Johnson was a fine actor and a real catch to get on the show. He had done many dramatic roles before joining our cast. He made all those scientific formulas and words he had to spout out sound perfectly authentic. And Dawn [Mary Ann] Wells was an unknown actress who answered a cattle call and auditioned with dozens and dozens of other actresses…including a then unknown Ann-Margret. But Dawn really stood out. She was so genuine and real and fit the part of the girl-next-door from Kansas perfectly. During the series' run, she got the most fan mail of all the cast.

"Jim [Thurston Howell] Backus suddenly became available six days before we were to film the beginning pilot episode. Since Jim was already an established actor, I knew he would be more expensive than our budget would allow. On the other hand, I knew that Hunt Stromberg [then vice president of programming at CBS] was very fond of Jim and would love to see him in *Gilligan's Island*. During casting, I told Hunt that Jim was my prototype for the role of Thurston Howell III. I knew Hunt agreed. Without hesitation, Hunt spoke for CBS. He said, 'Jim is perfect. You've got the extra money.' It was one of those many times Hunt helped me with the show."

And where would Thurston Howell have been without his Lovey?

"I remembered Natalie Schafer from dramatic films and the stage. But Hunt's father, Hunt Stromberg Sr., was an important film producer who had used Natalie in some of his movies. Hunt remembered she played high comedy very well. One meeting with Natalie was all it took. I was convinced I had my Lovey Howell.

"I remembered Tina [Ginger] Louise from a film *God's Little Acre*. She had a face and figure that were hard to forget. But she was in a Broadway musical at that moment when we were casting. The show was *Fade In, Fade Out* (starring Carol Burnett).

"In order for her to play Ginger, we had to buy out her contract for the balance of her guarantee to the musical. But it was well worth it. Even though Tina was not the easiest to work with at times, she was always a total pro when the camera was rolling. She later distanced herself from the series because she said it had typecast her. But she did show up for a full *Gilligan's Island* cast reunion on *The Late Show with Ross Shafer* in 1988."

What about the iconic opening theme song to the show? It seems most everyone over the age of forty can sing it by heart.

"The brass at CBS were concerned that when people tuned in each week, they wouldn't understand why or how this group was stranded on a desert island. So I came up with the idea of a theme song that would open the show each week and tell the story over again how it all came to be that they were stranded. I actually co-wrote the song with a gentleman named George Wyle."

To me, the most amazing story Sherwood told that day was about how *Gilligan's Island* was eventually canceled after three seasons. And it wasn't because of low ratings.

"In 1966, after a long run, *Gunsmoke* had fallen from the top twenty-five shows in the Nielsen ratings. So the CBS programming chiefs had taken it off the fall 1967 schedule. William Paley [founder of CBS] was furious. *Gunsmoke* was his favorite show of all time. It was also Mrs. Paley's favorite show. Mr. Paley wouldn't hear of dropping it from the schedule.

"The programmers went into emergency session to find a solution. Somebody in that meeting – and to this day no one will tell me who – came up with the idea of dropping a new half-hour sitcom that was scheduled for the fall but wasn't getting good response from the local stations to buy it. That show was scheduled to air after *Gilligan's Island*. If they dropped both the new show and Gilligan's Island, that would free up a full hour for the hour-long *Gunsmoke*. Mr. Paley liked the idea, and that was that. Even though I had been told a week earlier that *Gilligan* would get a fourth season that year, it never happened because of *Gunsmoke*."

Gilligan's Island never dropped out of the Nielsen Top 10 in its three-year run. But, as the old saying goes, "that's show business."

Although after three seasons, *Gilligan's Island* was unceremoniously canceled, its legacy wasn't over by a long shot. It has never been off the air since it was canceled…playing somewhere in the world (especially cable television). Thanks to reruns (and it's on DVD), the show has lived on and on. And that's to say nothing about the *Gilligan* TV specials that occurred in later years when the castaways were rescued. Plus, a fully animated TV series eventually happened. Sherwood Schwartz created a pop culture icon that continues to this day.

Although I could have talked on and on about *Gilligan*, I knew our time was limited so I shifted to The Brady Bunch. How did that show come about?

"Not long after *Gilligan* was up and running, I read an article in the *Los Angeles Times* that said 30 percent of marriages in the United States have a child or children from a previous marriage. That was around 1966. I can't imagine what that figure would be today. But in 1966, this was a new phenomenon. Television was loaded with happily married couples at that time, but I realized a whole new kind of family was springing up.

"So I started working on a script for a series tentatively titled *Yours and Mine*. I gave each parent three children and made the father a widower. I wanted the mother to be divorced, but the network was against that idea. We compromised by leaving Carol Brady's past open, so it was never made clear whether or not she was divorced or widowed.

"I shopped the series to the 'big three' networks of the time: ABC, CBS, and NBC. They all liked the script, but each network wanted changes before they would commit. So, for a while, I shelved the project.

"Then along came a film [in 1968] called *Yours, Mine and Ours* starring Henry Fonda and Lucille Ball. The film was a hit, and ABC remembered my script and ordered episodes for the series. We shot the show at Paramount, and it premiered in the fall of 1969.

"When *The Brady Bunch* – as it was finally called – got on the air, the producer of *Yours, Mine and Ours* threatened to sue Paramount for stealing the idea. Now, I had written the script for *The Brady Bunch* a good couple of years before the *Yours, Mine and Ours* script was done. So I called Paramount and said to them, 'Why don't you just have this gentleman go down to the Writer's Guild office and check out the registration date on my Brady script? And when he gets ahold of my script, you should also ask him to be grateful that *I* didn't sue *him*.' I said that because, as I said earlier, my original title on the script that would later become *The Brady Bunch* was *Yours and Mine*. We never heard from that producer again."

The Brady Bunch ran for five seasons, and the concept later became not one, but two successful Hollywood motion pictures. There were also numerous television specials and an animated series based on the concept. Once again, Sherwood Schwartz had created a pop culture icon.

Sherwood had generously given of his time to me, but I knew he had to get back to work after our long lunch on the very lot where *Gilligan's Island* had been filmed (yes, even as an octogenarian, he was still working!). But I had one final question.

"Can you take me over to the *Gilligan's Island* lagoon?" I asked.

"Sure," he agreed. "It's just steps away from here."

And two minutes later, I found myself standing at the edge of the lagoon where the characters Sherwood created had stood many times before, embroiled in some wacky adventure. Even though it was a parking lot, that didn't matter. Somehow, I could still hear Gilligan and the Skipper and the others trying to figure out how to get off that island.

If only they had known the Hollywood Freeway was just behind the palm trees. They could have hitched a ride.

15

OL' MAN VODKA

...it just kept rollin' along.

If you're familiar with the musical *Show Boat*, you'll know the chapter title is referencing the classic song "Ol' Man River" from that show. The lyric says, in effect, how Old Man River does indeed keep rolling along.

Show Boat was written by Jerome Kern and Oscar Hammerstein II and was a landmark in American musical theatre. It opened on Broadway in 1927, and compared to the trivial and unrealistic operettas, light musical comedies, and "Follies"-type musical revues that defined Broadway in the 1890s and the early twentieth century, *Show Boat* was a radical departure in musical storytelling, marrying spectacle and musical comedy with serious subjects. It laid the foundation for more landmark musicals to follow, such as Rodgers and Hammerstein's *Oklahoma!*

Meanwhile, we rewind to my days in Kentucky and the one hundredth anniversary of the birth of Jerome Kern that had rolled around (1985). I found out through the publicity surrounding Kern's birthday that his daughter, Betty Kern Miller, was living in Danville, Kentucky. I had been living in the state only a year at that time and didn't know exactly how far away Danville was, but I was going to find out. I figured Ms. Kern would have tons of great stories about not only her father but also the era in which he lived and the countless legends he rubbed elbows with. So I got on the phone to track her down (here we go again).

My detective work finally led me to her personal assistant, Craig. He said he was getting a lot of requests for interviews with Mrs. Miller due to the one hundredth anniversary hoopla, and he was reluctant to let me speak to her. I gently persisted, and I finally hit on what unlocked the door.

"I conducted the pit orchestra for her father's musical *Show Boat* a few summers ago," I said. "I really enjoyed getting to know that score. It's incredible." (And I meant every word of it.)

"Oh, that's very interesting," said her assistant. "None of the other people from the media calling to interview Mrs. Miller really know her father's music, and she seems a bit put off by that."

I felt him starting to soften a bit.

"Tell you what," he said. I'll mention to Mrs. Miller that you've called, and if she's interested in speaking with you, she'll give you a call in the next few days."

That was good enough for me. I was thrilled that he didn't shut me down immediately.

The next morning, my phone rang, and it was none other than Betty Kern Miller. Her voice was somewhat throaty and elegant, exactly as I would have expected her to sound.

"Mark, I understand you would like to come to Danville and interview me about my father," she said.

"Absolutely, Mrs. Miller. I would be honored."

She seemed slightly reticent, and I could already detect that she had a feisty nature. Which didn't deter me one bit actually.

"Craig tells me that you know my father's music. What are some of your favorite songs he wrote?" she quizzed.

"Well, anything from *Show Boat*. I conducted the pit orchestra for a production of that show a few summers ago. And of course several of his other classics such as 'All the Things You Are' and 'Smoke Gets in Your Eyes.'"

Bull's-eye. Her voice lightened up when she knew I was a certified and knowledgeable fan of her father. We then chatted for another three or four minutes about Jerome Kern's music. Suddenly, she offered, "When would you like to come to Danville?"

I wasted no time. "What about this Friday?"

"Oh, I can't meet during that day. I've a horse event to attend," she replied.

A "horse event"? What the…? I later found out that Mrs. Miller owned Silver Lining Stables, a thoroughbred horse breeding farm (named after her father's song "Look for the Silver Lining" made famous by various singers and later, a Hollywood motion picture). Danville was in the eastern part of Kentucky, the true bluegrass area, and a bastion of thoroughbred horse racing and breeding (naturally, since it is near Louisville – home of the venerable Kentucky Derby).

Then she had an impromptu idea. "But you, Craig, and I could have dinner Friday evening, following my event. Afterward, we can come back to my home and chat."

I was thrilled. Sounded like a possibly wonderful evening afoot.

"That's terrific. I'll then spend Friday night in Danville and drive back to Owensboro on Saturday. Do you have any suggested hotels near your home?"

Then I was amazed by what she offered somewhat matter-of-factly: "No, no. You won't need a hotel. You can stay here in my guest house."

My, oh, my! I had gone from being a stranger to receiving an invitation to stay in Jerome Kern's daughter's guest house in the thoroughbred horse racing capital of the world. I was somewhat taken aback and certainly flattered. "I'll be there!" I said before she could change her mind.

It was Friday before I knew it, and I was making the three-hour trip from Owensboro to Danville. I could tell Danville was a beautiful, staid, and "old money" town when I rolled in that evening. Mrs. Miller's neighborhood was stunning, and her home was pure old-style Kentucky class and beauty. It was a three-story stately mansion, lit nicely for the evening. I walked up to the front door and rang the bell.

I was greeted by a housekeeper, who led me into a sitting area. Soon, Mrs. Miller and her assistant, Craig, emerged. She looked to be in her early- to mid-seventies, and I could tell she was extremely polished and savvy. We soon were off to the restaurant for a nice dinner.

After dinner, we went back to Mrs. Miller's home, and Craig retired to another part of the house. Mrs. Miller and I settled into the music library, which contained a beautiful grand piano (her father's, she said). I dared not even touch it. The library wasn't just filled with books, but original manuscripts from Jerome Kern himself. Here were housed the actual, original manuscripts to some of the most famous songs in the world heard and sung by millions over the years (to say nothing of the millions of dollars they generated).

We sat down, and I pulled out a tape recorder I'd brought to document our conversations.

"What's that?" she asked.

Certainly this seventy-something lady of polish and refinement knew what a tape recorder was. I detected her feisty back going up a bit at the prospect I was going to record everything we said, so I responded nonchalantly: "Oh, it's just a little tape recorder. I want to get everything down accurately."

I could tell she didn't like the idea, but she didn't push back anymore. At least not yet.

I opened with my first question, cliché as it was: "What was it like growing up with Jerome Kern as your father?"

"I don't really know. It's the only thing I knew. All these other reporters who have been trying to interview me about him all ask if I loved him or not. Well, of course I loved my father. I adored him."

I sensed a slight defensiveness in her answer. Seems as if a lot of others had been trying to dig for some dirt. I didn't want dirt. I just wanted fun stories. And ever since I'd brought out the tape recorder, her demeanor had changed. She was more guarded. And she kept glancing at it. Finally, she could take it no more.

"Is it really necessary to have that recorder?"

I knew I had to make a decision. Either have all of her comments carefully documented forever verbatim or risk dampening an entire once-in-a-lifetime evening with the daughter of Jerome Kern. I knew what I had to do.

"Absolutely not. If this makes you the slightest bit uncomfortable, I will turn it off and put it away." Which I did. She relaxed immediately.

What followed were endless stories about everyone from George ("Georgy" as she called him) and Ira Gershwin to Frank Sinatra to Richard Rodgers and Oscar Hammerstein. Her stories were so vivid, it was as if Cole Porter, Hoagy Carmichael, Johnny Mercer, and friends had walked into the room that night to join us. In addition, Mrs. Miller had been married at one time to famed bandleader-clarinetist Artie Shaw. (Who wasn't? Artie Shaw was married a total of eight times, including Lana Turner and Ava Gardner. Betty Kern was his fourth wife, and they were married for a whole year – longer than some of Shaw's other marriages. The union produced a son, Steven.)

Early in the evening, Mrs. Miller offered me a drink. Not a Sprite, mind you, but a mixed drink. She was having vodka and grapefruit juice and offered me the same.

Now, I'm not much of a real drinker. I'll have a glass of wine every month or so with dinner and friends but not mixed drinks. Here was a Hollywood pro who had been around the block a time or two, and this was simply part of the routine. Not being one to poop the party (and I was certainly curious about what vodka and grapefruit juice tasted like), I said, "Sure."

We started talking around 7:00 p.m. We finished at 6:45 a.m. We talked all night, and we drank vodka and grapefruit juice *all night!* If she said it once, she said it a thousand times: "Let me freshen your drink." The beautiful grandfather clock in the hallway seemed to chime every ten minutes, not every hour.

To this day, that is one of the two times in my life I've stayed up and awake all night (the other was when I was writing orchestrations for a musical and was up against a deadline). Of course, the bulk of our conversations focused on her father. And for those readers who aren't completely acquainted with his illustrious career, here is a bit about him.

Jerome Kern was one of the most important American theatre composers of the early twentieth century. He wrote more than seven hundred songs, used in more than one hundred stage works, including such classics as "Can't Help Lovin' Dat Man," "A Fine Romance," "Smoke Gets in Your Eyes," "All the Things You Are," "The Way You Look Tonight," "Long Ago (and Far Away)," and "Who?" He collaborated with many of the leading librettists and lyricists of his era, including Ira Gershwin, Johnny Mercer, Oscar Hammerstein II, George Grossmith Jr., Guy Bolton, P. G. Wodehouse, Dorothy Fields, Otto Harbach, and E. Y. Harburg.

A native New Yorker, Kern created dozens of Broadway musicals and Hollywood films in a career that lasted more than four decades. His musical innovations, such as 4/4 dance rhythms and the employment of syncopation and jazz progressions, built on, rather than rejected, earlier musical theatre tradition. He and his collaborators also employed his melodies to further the action or develop characterization to a greater extent than in the other musicals of his day, creating the model for later musicals.

Although dozens of Kern's musicals and musical films were hits, only *Show Boat* is now regularly revived. Songs from his other shows, however, are still frequently performed and adapted. Although Kern detested jazz arrangements of his songs, many have been adopted by jazz musicians to become standard tunes.

At one point during our very long conversation, Mrs. Miller took me into one part of the library where she showed me several original Kern manuscripts, which I held and examined. One I'll never forget was the original manuscript for *Show Boat*. It still had Kern's personal notes scribbled in the margins.

If that weren't enough, around 4:00 a.m. (after several drink freshenings and the party was in full swing), she led me over to his piano and suggested I play a few songs (by then, she knew that I played piano). Of course I did and couldn't resist playing Kern's immortal "Ol' Man River"– reading from Kern's original manuscript – on the piano Mrs. Miller said he wrote it! Now, *that* was a moment.

I looked up at the grandfather clock in the hallway. It read 6:45 a.m. Betty (we were certainly on a first-name basis by then) seemed fresh as a daisy. Good gosh, this refined and polished lady turned out to be a showbiz broad who could hold her liquor. I was deliriously drunk. It had happened so slowly, I didn't even see it coming. I couldn't make it to the guest house. She said I could go upstairs to the guest quarters. I managed to get there and pour myself into bed.

Around two o'clock that afternoon, I awoke to the downstairs clock chiming. It sounded like Big Ben in my head! Then the phone rang. Again, it was as if someone was banging my head inside Jerome Kern's piano. For the next twenty minutes, I struggled to *sit up* in the bed. Getting my feet on the floor was not something that I even contemplated yet. If I could just sit up, possibly life would continue. *Note to young and old readers alike: Do not try this at home! Or anywhere!*

Finally, I was sitting up. *Now*, I thought, *the ultimate challenge of putting my feet on the floor.*

Another twenty minutes later, mission accomplished! And then, I graduated to *standing up*!

That was short-lived, and I tumbled back on the bed. Another fifteen minutes later, I was again standing and this time actually moving to put on my clothing.

I eventually made my way downstairs to the kitchen where fresh-as-a-daisy Betty was drinking coffee and reading the newspaper as the housekeeper whipped up breakfast or brunch or lunch or whatever it was at that time under those circumstances. Betty was unfazed by the night before.

"How did you sleep?" she asked. Her voice sounded like she was a giant from a Grimm's fairy tale as it echoed in my head.

"Oh, I don't remember. I think I must have slept fine."

"Well, I do wish those reporters from *Time* magazine would stop calling me. And the *New York Times* as well. Both called back again this morning and wanted to speak to me again, and I just don't want to talk to them," she said.

Although her voice was still punishing my very psyche, I was stunned at the realization that while *Time* magazine and the *New York Times* couldn't get the time of day with her, I had just spent the night in her home and talked all night with her. In that moment, the pain was worth every bit of it!

After I got some food on my stomach, I was starting to regain my strength and feel a bit normal again. Betty said she needed to stop by her Silver Lining Stables and asked if I would like to join her.

"Absolutely," I said. (Little did she know that I imagined my going with her would require another month's worth of sleep, a hospital stay, and millions of dollars of reconstructive surgery.)

So off we went to see some of her thoroughbred horses galloping through the Kentucky bluegrass. It was quite another moment, remembering that she'd told me during our long conversation the night before that her father enjoyed horse racing. Perhaps that was why she was now drawn to horses, since she grew up around them.

After about an hour at the farm, I knew it was time for me to make my way back home. I hugged her and thanked her for an unforgettable time. She seemed appreciative of our time together as well, and that made me happy. As I drove away, I took one last look. She was feeding one of her horses an apple. I later heard that horse ran in the Kentucky Derby that year.

Betty Kern Miller died eleven years later. Other than a thank-you letter I sent to her, I never saw or communicated with her again. But what a night with Jerome Kern, Cole Porter, Rodgers and Hammerstein, and the Gershwins! And of course, ol' man vodka (whom I *never* want to see again).

16

THE END OF SHAWNEE PRESS, INC.

As I've said, I consider the phone one of my best friends. Indeed, I'm on a first-name basis with it, and as you've seen, it's often been a willing accomplice in helping execute my "what-if" dreams. However, sometimes that friend has reached out and touched me in unwanted and surprising ways. I'll bet for you too.

Case in point: One afternoon in March 2009, my friend the phone rang in my office at Shawnee Press. It was Barrie Edwards calling from his new office in Santa Monica, California. (Bob Wise had moved Barrie and much of the New York office staff out there to be closer to the film and TV business as they pitched songs to be used in those mediums.) Barrie was his usual cordial self and said that he wanted me to come to California as soon as possible because he had something to tell me.

Something to tell me? That required me to fly to California? I wondered. My heart skipped a few beats.

"Is everything okay?" I asked.

"Oh, fine…nothing to be worried about, but I would like to chat with you about it over dinner," he said.

"Sure," I replied, trying to match his calm tone.

I reminded him I had a trip to New York scheduled for the upcoming weekend. He suggested I fly from New York to Los Angeles on Sunday, and we could have dinner that evening in Santa Monica. He would make hotel reservations for me. I said that sounded fine and booked the flight.

I didn't sleep very well for the next several nights. I got on the plane that Friday for my trip to New York. The visit to New York was fine, even if a pall of mystery hung over the proceedings. As usual on a trip to NYC, I had a meal with Buryl Red (more on him in a later chapter) and confided in him what was happening. He found it curious as well and corroborated the several possible scenarios I had conjured up about why Barrie had summoned me to California: they were selling the company; he was retiring; Bob was ill; his dog was sick; he had a hangnail! I would have thrown in the possibility Barrie was firing me – and that thought certainly crossed my mind – but held to the fact that he'd said everything was "fine," and I couldn't see how he could classify things that way if, indeed, I was going to get a pink slip. Besides, sales at Shawnee Press were up and had continually been up year after year since the new team took over. And yet visions of Fred Waring and Ernie and Marjorie Farmer danced in my head.

I arrived at the sleek beachside Santa Monica hotel where Barrie had booked me and changed for dinner. At last, 6:00 p.m. Pacific time arrived, and I got on the elevator to go down to the restaurant. Those types of days are always the longest when you fly from the East Coast to the West coast and gain three hours. Although the clock said 6:00 p.m., my body was telling me it was 9:00 p.m. But that didn't matter. The adrenaline was flowing, and I was anxious to find out what was going on. I saw Barrie immediately when I stepped into the lobby, and we walked a few steps to the hotel restaurant.

We sat at the table and made the usual opening small talk. He reminisced for a few moments about my early days at Shawnee and staying in the Shawnee Inn for three months. After the waiter poured the water into our glasses, Barrie's expression became a bit more serious. I hoped he would, at long last, reveal what required me to be summoned all the way to California, which certainly had to be more significant than a nice dinner in Santa Monica.

He spoke, "I think you should take the Word job."

From the same mouth that had uttered eight words that had changed my life more than four years earlier ("What would you think about running Shawnee Press?") now came eight *new* words that would again alter the course of my career (and the same for several others) forever.

Okay…rewind to two months before this night. I had been approached by Word Entertainment to head up Word Music, their print music division, filling the shoes left by Don Cason (who had been at Word for twenty-eight years). Due to Word's rocky road (for various reasons) over the last several years, Don had been let go over a year prior, and the print music grapevine said that things were not going well for Word Music these days. Since the print music business is relatively very small (and the sacred print music business even smaller), I didn't want Barrie to find out secondhand that I had been approached by Word and might be considering leaving Shawnee, so I had proactively told him about the Word offer about a month before this night.

The thoughts immediately came rushing to me as I sat there dumbfounded: *"What? Take the job at Word? What do you mean? Why should I take the job at Word? I don't want to take the job at Word. I like Shawnee Press. I want to retire there and even try to buy it someday."*

Finally, I spoke: "Why should I take the job at Word?"

"Bob has decided to get out of the print music business. He's made a deal with Hal Leonard, and they're going to become the print publisher for Music Sales. And that includes Shawnee Press."

I was stunned. My mind was reeling. I still hadn't absorbed it all.

Barrie proceeded to tell me that a secret deal was in the works – and had been for a while now – with Hal Leonard. Against all the insiders' wishes, Barrie was telling me their secret plan. Everyone wanted this deal very locked down and kept quiet, and that even included not telling me about it. Understandably, they wanted everything to keep perking along until the deal was closed. Yet Barrie didn't want me to pass up a potential opportunity for continued gainful employment, in this case with Word, as

Hal Leonard would most likely combine all of Shawnee's operations with its own, thus eliminating several positions, probably including mine. And I will always be grateful he gave me that "heads up."

It was starting to sink in, and unfortunately, it made sense. When Bob Wise had purchased the venerable G. Schirmer years before, he immediately licensed the print rights to Hal Leonard – not even to his own print music company or Shawnee Press at the time. The bottom had dropped out of the economy in the fall of 2008, and everyone's sales were suffering…people were being laid off right and left, and companies were looking to economize. And although this downturn had hit Music Sales hard on the print side, Shawnee was holding steady. It made sense, then, when Barrie said he thought Shawnee was the plum that Hal Leonard wanted. It would deepen their share of the church music market, while simultaneously eliminating a competitor. Plus, such a deal with Hal Leonard would bring Bob's entire music print operation (including G. Schirmer) into one place: Hal Leonard. Such deals happen all the time in the music business (and other businesses, of course), and one can never blame another publisher for wanting to grow and acquire more market share through acquisition. It's simply how the business works.

Nevertheless, I felt like a boxer who had been knocked to the mat. But as the meal continued and I barely touched my food, I started to come back around, regain my footing, and get up off the mat.

"Would Bob consider selling Shawnee Press to me?" I asked.

Barrie paused, thought a bit, and then said, "Maybe."

We finished our dinner. Barrie encouraged me to stay another day in Santa Monica and relax and enjoy the beach if I wanted to. But I was determined to get back to Nashville and start working on a plan to somehow acquire Shawnee Press.

When I returned to my hotel room and continued to "thaw" from the news he'd told me, my mind flashed back to an important budget meeting about a year before in New York with the Music Sales management team, including Bob Wise. They were suddenly no longer concerned with top-line sales increases (which Bob stressed since Day One with me – and we had achieved), but bottom-line performance. The earlier edict from Bob in my first meeting with him four years earlier to "make Shawnee grow" had now become "make Shawnee more profitable."

I later learned from a few industry insiders that Bob had probably intended to sell Shawnee Press for some time, and I was possibly there to pump it up and get it ready for to be an attractive acquisition for someone. Who knows? Bob was always very cordial and supportive in my years there. Regardless, the next morning, from the Los Angeles airport, I called Jim Van Hook from my cell phone.

"You're not going to believe this, Jim," I said.

"You're in prison," he replied.

We laughed, and then I told him what Barrie had revealed to me about Shawnee Press the night before and that he thought Bob Wise would be willing to entertain an offer from me to buy it. Jim was intrigued and offered to set up a meeting with me and a Nashville attorney (Kurt Beasley) who specialized in music publishing catalog acquisitions. As usual, Jim was good to his word, and he, Kurt, and I were sitting at lunch the next week.

The next four weeks were filled with countless e-mails, phone calls, and meetings between me and Kurt to assess Shawnee's numbers and selling price that Barrie had quoted to me. We pushed, pulled, and crunched, but nothing was working. It was just priced too high, according to Kurt.

I was driving home one Friday afternoon in April, and Kurt called: "We've done a final pass of the numbers, Mark, and if you're going to have a prayer of making this work, you'll need to bring in some sort of partner who has distribution services built in."

My mind immediately rewound to a conversation I'd had with Reiff Lorenz a few years earlier at a conference we were attending. He is part of the Lorenz family dynasty that has owned the Lorenz Corporation (music publishers) since its inception well over one hundred years ago. I like and respect Reiff and the entire Lorenz family. Lorenz (the company) had been stable and growing (as far as I could tell) over the years. During that casual conversation with him those few years earlier, Reiff said that if I ever wanted to start my own company, he hoped that I would give him a call.

I figured now was the time to do so.

That night…a Friday, no less, I tracked Reiff down and called him at his home. I told him of the situation and asked if Lorenz would like to consider buying Shawnee Press with me. He was immediately interested and encouraged me to come to Dayton, Ohio, where the company had been based all these many years, as soon as possible. I booked a flight that night from Nashville to Dayton for the following Monday morning.

When I arrived in Dayton, Reiff picked me up at the airport and took me to a nice lunch. We brainstormed about the possibilities. Afterward, he took me to the Lorenz headquarters in downtown Dayton and gave me a tour of the cavernous building. It appeared as I would expect for a more than one-hundred-year-old company. Despite its large size, it isn't the most impressive facility in the world. But I could tell it is extremely efficient, and that's what matters most (and has certainly helped keep them in the business successfully for so long). Besides, I'd learned many years ago and noted earlier when I first laid eyes on Shawnee Press, music publishers needn't be housed in fancy and modern buildings to be successful (as a matter of fact, that's often a key to their success).

Reiff and I then settled into a conference room where he had all the Shawnee numbers loaded into his laptop computer and projected on a large screen for us to review. For two hours, we jiggled, crunched, and pushed numbers, all based on what was the immovable Shawnee selling price, despite some attempted dickering on my part with Barrie Edwards.

Nothing worked. It was just overpriced. And everyone—Kurt Beasley and his team, Jim Van Hook, and now Reiff—agreed.

He took me back to the Dayton airport. As we were saying our good-byes, Reiff asked, "What are you going to do?" I said simply, "Take the job at Word."

As a final "Hail Mary pass," I called Barrie Edwards from the Dayton airport and gave him the number that Reiff and I knew would work in the formulas we had determined as to what we could offer for Shawnee Press. Barrie tactfully declined, saying that he knew they could get their selling price from Hal Leonard.

They did.

When Music Sales Corporation purchased Shawnee Press in 1989, Shawnee had forty-seven employees. When I became the head of Shawnee in 2005, the company had eight employees. Of course, some of that reduction was understandable. Music Sales provided warehousing, shipping, copyright administration, and other back office functions for Shawnee that Shawnee did on its own before being acquired.

When Shawnee was acquired by Hal Leonard Corporation in 2009, the reduction continued, as predicted (and is usual in these deals). Shawnee was dissolved as a corporation and became an imprint of Hal Leonard. As of this writing, there are no employees who devote full-time work to Shawnee Press anymore. So it went from forty-seven employees to zero in a twenty-year period.

That's stunning when you think of the heyday the company enjoyed once upon a time. And while I do lament the basic disappearance of Shawnee Press, I write this paragraph not as an indictment but as an education about how change in the music business (and other industries, for that matter) is inevitable—for better or worse. It certainly happens all the time (for example, long-time toy company Fisher-Price was acquired by rival Mattel; Pillsbury was acquired by rival General Mills, etc.). The same thing can be said of Brentwood Music.

But for those of us who remember "the way it was" (especially including all those years long before I arrived on the scene), we sometimes pause with that bittersweet sigh of reminiscence. But as my beloved high school choral director, Helen Krause, always says: "The only thing permanent in this world is change."

Indeed.

JAMES BOND MEETS JAMES WEST

What could the wacky comedy *Gilligan's Island* possibly have in common with the Wild West?

Not far from *Gilligan's Island* on the CBS Studio Center lot, another show was produced there once upon a time. Some readers will remember it; others will not. But in its day, it was a big hit on CBS and is still seen on cable TV these days. The show was *The Wild Wild West.*

As a kid, I loved the show. It was a different kind of western. It ran for four seasons from 1965 to 1969. Two television movies were made with the original cast in 1979 and 1980, and the series was adapted as a major motion picture (starring Will Smith and Kevin Kline) in 1999.

And one sunny day in Los Angeles at a restaurant right up the street from CBS Studio Center, I found myself sitting across the table having lunch with none other than the star of *The Wild Wild West*—Robert Conrad.

Developed at a time when the television western was losing ground to the spy genre, the show was conceived as "James Bond on a horse." Set during the administration of President Ulysses Grant, the series followed Secret Service agents James West (Conrad), a fearless and smooth operator; and Artemus Gordon (Ross Martin), a brilliant gadgeteer and master of disguise. They solved crimes, protected the president, and foiled the plans of megalomaniacal villains to take over all or part of the United States.

The show also featured a number of fantasy elements, such as the technologically advanced devices used by the agents and their adversaries. The combination of the Victorian era time frame and the use of Jules Verne-esque style technology have inspired some to give the show credit for the origins of the steam punk subculture. These elements were accentuated even more in the 1999 movie adaptation.

Once again, I was casting about for radio show guests, and being the fan of *The Wild Wild West* and Robert Conrad that I was, I thought with my usual "What the heck?" approach that it would be fun to meet Mr. Conrad. So after a few phone calls to my contacts in Los Angeles (I am dangerous with a phone!), I got to Conrad's agent and then to Conrad himself. He agreed to have lunch with me for an interview.

When I walked into the restaurant, he was easy to spot. Several women had gathered around him to ask for his autograph, and he was charming every one of them. Just like his Jim West character.

We settled into lunch, and I got out my dependable hand-held tape recorder. I was looking forward to hearing the behind-the-scenes scoop of his work and career. So how did he get started in show business?

Born Conrad Robert Falk (and one can obviously see how he adapted his birth name for his stage name), he grew up in Chicago. "I then went to New York to become an actor. Next, I came to Hollywood in 1957. A few years after getting to LA, I was offered a part on an ABC-TV show called *Hawaiian Eye*," said Robert.

"Was that a good experience?" I asked.

"Oh, yeah. I got to do some shooting in Hawaii, and I learned how to surf while I was there working on the series."

Hawaiian Eye was one of several ABC-TV detective series of the era situated in different exotic locales. Others included Hollywood-based *77 Sunset Strip*, *Bourbon Street Beat* set in New Orleans, and Miami's *Surfside*

Six. The show lasted four seasons, then Robert said he was filming a movie when an opportunity for another series came along.

"I was doing a movie called *Young Dillinger* when my agent called and said CBS was testing for a big television series and I was number seventeen to audition. I asked my agent, 'Is this audition really necessary? If they've got at least seventeen guys, surely one of them has a big name and will get the part before me.' He said, 'You've got a name from *Hawaiian Eye*.' Well, I got the part, and they said I needed to be in wardrobe the very next day and that we'd be filming in Jamestown [CA] on Monday. So things went fast."

That role was for James West in *The Wild Wild West*—the series that made Conrad a star. But who had the idea to put "James Bond on a horse"?

"Mike Garrison was a very talented and creative guy who created the series. The show went through several changes in producers in its first season. This was due to conflicts between the network and Garrison, who had no experience producing for television and had trouble staying on budget.

"Very unfortunately, Mike died while we were filming the first season. Then Bruce Lansbury took over. Bruce was a great filmmaker. His sister is the legendary Angela Lansbury. Their brother is a Broadway producer – Edgar [*Godspell*]. Leonard Katzman was also involved. He left and went to *Gunsmoke* and then on to the show *Dallas*."

So what were some of his best memories of the series? I asked next.

"We had a six-day filming schedule to do each show. Nowadays, they take eight days to do shows of that type. So it was a tight schedule."

I couldn't help making the connection that *West* was filmed at Studio Center where other famous shows of that era were filmed. Was he friendly with other stars from other shows on the lot at the time?

"*Rawhide* with Clint Eastwood was filmed there at that time. Clint was a nice guy and always friendly. Then there was also that comedy with the kid on the island…*Gilligan's Island*. That was shot near us. I got to know Alan Hale [the Skipper] well. He was a great guy, and we often had lunch together across the street from the studio. Oh, and there was also

Gunsmoke that filmed there at the time. Jim Arness [Marshal Dillon] was a class act."

"Ross Martin seemed like a wonderful person. What was he like to work with?" I asked.

"We were best friends. He loved the acting, and I loved the action. It was casting made in heaven for the network. He was a classy guy. We actually didn't have a lot in common, however. For example, I would go to the Olympic Auditorium in Los Angeles to watch boxing, and he would go to the theatre or opera on Friday. He spoke five languages fluently, and I have trouble with English."

Ross Martin died in Los Angeles while playing tennis at age sixty-one in 1981.

"He left us way too soon," said Robert. "We got along, and it showed up on film. We didn't take it too seriously. Ross was always in some funny costume. It was great."

I couldn't resist asking about the man who had to be the most eccentric and popular villain of all time on the show—the diminutive Dr. Lovelace (played by Michael Dunn).

"Dr. Lovelace was my favorite character in the series," Conrad said.

"Michael was from New York, and he used to stay at my house when he came to Los Angeles to shoot the show. We used to play a Saturday football game called 'contact touch' after we finished shooting that week's episode. Each week's cast—including any male guest stars—were invited to play along with us regulars. The best hit I ever got was from Lee Majors [television's *Six Million Dollar Man*]. I congratulated him because it was a perfect shot. Michael Dunn would referee. He was three feet eight inches, and we used to put him in a golf cart refereeing the game. Every Saturday we played. We'd go to a bar afterwards and continue the fun."

Robert was animated and clearly enjoying remembering Dunn.

"I liked it when Michael wanted to do his own stunts. He always said he didn't want another dwarf doubling him on his stunts. There was one show when he was in a small coal mining car on a railroad track. Somehow, something went wrong, and the car ran off the track while he was still in it. He really got banged up pretty badly and had to be hospitalized for a few days.

"That Saturday, we didn't play our usual football game and instead went to see Michael in the hospital. We made him an honorary member of the Stuntmen's Association. He said he was the only dwarf in the Stuntmen's Association, and I said, 'Yeah, and I'm the only actor.' And he said, 'I've seen your work, Bob, and you're not an actor.' And I said, 'Thank you very much, you little SOB.' We had a big laugh over it."

"Speaking of stunts," I followed up, "is it true you did some of your own stunts as well?"

"I actually did all of my own stunts. But there was a price to be paid for that. I broke my skull on January 23, 1968, doing a particularly complicated one. But I didn't stop doing my own stunts after that. Maybe I damaged my brain so much when I broke my skull that I didn't have sense enough to stop doing them!"

I was loving every minute of this. What other memories did he have of the show?

"It was always fun to come to work. The last year I didn't read the scripts because I knew what to expect from the writers. Always quality material."

Anything else?

"My tight pants always ripped. The CBS costume department kept having to make new ones each week," he said with a laugh.

Despite the fact that *The Wild Wild West* had some of the highest ratings in television during its run—even its last season—it was canceled by CBS as "a concession to Congress over television violence," he said.

"There was a senator from Rhode Island who was a watchdog about television violence," he explained. "Some at the network considered putting it in a later time slot to get it away from kids seeing it. But the network didn't think the show would do well in a later time period. So they canceled it because they didn't think it could sustain its high ratings at ten at night…they saw the audience as being primarily young, but the demographic was primarily college students and up."

It was the end of a great show. But fortunately, it lives on in reruns and a home DVD release of the entire series (for which Conrad provided special introductions and commentaries).

Any actor would be thankful to have one hit network series in a career, but Conrad is in that rare group who has had not one – but *three* (including *Hawaiian Eye*)—to his credit. The third was *Baa Baa Black Sheep* (later titled *Black Sheep Squadron*).

So how did lightning strike the third time for Conrad?

"*Baa Baa Black Sheep* came about because of a book, which was written by Greg ["Pappy"] Boyington," he explained. "Greg sold the concept to Universal and they had a hot writer named Stephen Cannell and they asked him if he would like to develop it for TV and Cannell said, 'Yes.'"

Stephen J. Cannell went on to create or co-create nearly forty television series, mostly crime dramas including *The Rockford Files, The Greatest American Hero, The A-Team, Hardcastle & McCormick, Wiseguy, 21 Jump Street, Silk Stalkings*, and *The Commish*.

"*Baa Baa Black Sheep* had a similar fate as *The Wild Wild West*," Conrad added.

"In what way?" I was curious to know.

"The show had the largest male audience in the history of television. The advertisers loved that because the male audience is harder to capture than the female audience—other than with sports programming. Ratings were strong for the show.

"But it got canceled because of an organization called Mothers Against Violence on Television. The producers were using actual aerial shots from the Marine Corps film library, which contained actual footage of troops. The moms said that was too realistic. So after two successful seasons, the show was canceled."

There was one final success I wanted to mention to him, and that was the critical acclaim he received for *Centennial*, the 1978–79 NBC miniseries. It was based on the novel of the same name by the legendary James A. Michener.

"*Centennial* was a great experience based on James Michener's quality book. I got a nice note from Michener about the show. That meant more to me than just about anything," he said with a smile.

Our time was coming to a close. We had finished our dessert, and I knew I had to let "Mr. West" get back to his next project (he was directing a film at Paramount that day). (Side note: I will add that of all the celebrities I've known and worked with over the years, next to Shirley Jones, Robert Conrad was also very close to his television personas. What you see is what you get.)

It struck me that Robert probably would have known the late, legendary William S. Paley, founder of CBS.

"Oh, sure, I knew Bill Paley. He was a nice guy. And of course a brilliant businessman and television pioneer. But he hated the dwarf."

"I beg your pardon?" I said.

"The Dr. Lovelace character on *The Wild Wild West*. Paley didn't get that character and asked the producers if they might stop using it in the show. But the writers persisted and won that point. And I'm glad they did."

He added with a wink, "Otherwise, who would have refereed our football games on Saturday?"

18

HI-HO, STEVERINO!

The entertainment legend walked over to his piano, sat down, and started to play.

The song was immediately familiar to me. I sat on the couch beside the piano and thought: *I can't believe I'm having a private audience with one of my heroes.* And he was not only one of my heroes but also a hero to millions of others.

As he played, I sang the lyrics softly. The song was "This Could Be the Start of Something Big," and he had written it. It been heard by millions over the years and become what is called in the music business a "standard" and had been recorded by numerous artists through the years, including Count Basie, Tony Bennett, Bobby Darin, Ella Fitzgerald, Judy Garland, Aretha Franklin, Lionel Hampton, Steve Lawrence and Eydie Gormé, Oscar Peterson, and more (there's a whole string of bonus name-dropping for you!).

The songwriter/pianist that day was none other than Steve Allen. And I was sitting in his Hollywood office working on a project with him. More on that later. But first, for those readers who remember Steve, they know he was far more than a pianist and songwriter (although he was so prolific as a songwriter – having written more than 8,500 songs – he was listed in the 1985 *Guinness Book of World Records* as the world's most prolific songwriter and won a coveted Grammy Award for best jazz composition with his song "The Gravy Waltz"). He also wrote lyrics for the standards "Picnic" and "South Rampart Street Parade."

Some readers may be too young to remember Steve. But that's a big part of my purpose in writing this book: To introduce readers unfamiliar with these talented and incredible people, as well as celebrate these individuals on a personal level with those who are familiar with them. I suggest you go to YouTube (www.youtube.com) and enter Steve Allen's name in the search engine. You'll be amazed and highly entertained by this true genius. (By the way, I've learned to see YouTube as a wonderful repository of great, historic entertainment treasures and not just a place where you see little clips of a friend's birthday party...although those are important too.)

Before Johnny Carson, Jack Paar, Jay Leno, Jimmy Kimmel, or Jimmy Fallon, there was Steve. As the very first host of *The Tonight Show* on NBC-TV in 1954, Steve set the pace for the show that has become America's longest-running and most successful late night program. The format seems inevitable now: the monologue, the band, the desk, the celebrities. But it was Steve Allen who invented this formula. Steve was doing the crazy stunts, audience chat, man-on-the-street interviews, and more that Jay Leno, David Letterman, and Jimmy Fallon are doing now. To their great credit, I've heard all of these hosts, at various times, pay tribute to Steve as one of their heroes and a pioneer in the field of late night television. As Jay Leno is quoted as saying, "There's nothing new. It all started with Steve." Allen made a final appearance on *The Tonight Show* on September 27, 1994, for the show's fortieth anniversary broadcast. Jay was effusive in praise and actually knelt down and kissed his ring.

Though he got his start in radio, Steve is best known for his television career. He first gained national attention as a guest host on *Arthur Godfrey's Talent Scouts*. He then graduated to host *The Tonight Show*. Thereafter, he hosted numerous game and variety shows, including *The*

Steve Allen Show, I've Got a Secret, and *The New Steve Allen Show,* and he was a regular panelist on CBS-TV's *What's My Line?*

Two celebrities in particular caught my attention and imagination in my mid-twenties: Meredith Willson and Steve Allen. The reason I became fascinated (and inspired) by them is that in addition to having very successful careers, they did all the things in which I was – and am – interested: Music (publishing, performing, composing, and conducting), broadcasting, and writing (books and other things). And they both did all of these things at a very high level. As for Steve Allen, here was the true embodiment of a *Renaissance man.*

So how did I end up sitting in Steve Allen's office on Burbank Boulevard? As usual, it all started with a "what-if" moment and then a phone call.

My friend Loonis McGlohon (whom you'll meet later in this book) had co-produced and participated in an hour-long radio program (with Charles Kuralt) for National Public Radio (NPR) titled *Our Funny Valentines.* It aired on Valentine's Day evening (1996) coast to coast and featured Charles Kuralt reading lyrics to great American popular love songs by Rodgers and Hart, Cole Porter, the Gershwins, and others…all underscored by Loonis at the piano as they commented on each composer and lyric. The show was a hit, and ever the champion of *American popular song,* Loonis encouraged me to explore other ideas that might be produced for NPR along those lines.

I had been a lifelong fan of the great Steve Allen, and my "what-if" moment converged into me wondering: *What if I could get in touch with Steve and have him host a show for NPR, which I would write and produce, titled Steve Allen's Great American Songwriters? And most important, I would get to spend quality time learning from this legend.*

My mantra of "Nothing ventured, nothing gained" popped up once again. I had nothing to lose. It seemed like a long shot, but so what? At the very least I would get to speak to Mr. Allen and tell him how his life and career had so greatly inspired me.

Little did I know that "what-if" moment would lead to a lot of obstacles to make it happen. But as the old saying goes, anything that's worth doing is not only worth doing well, it's usually not going to be easy.

And it wasn't.

After digging around with my music biz contacts and obtaining a phone number for Steve, I gathered my courage and called him. After finally getting through a few assistants, I got him on the phone.

"Mr. Allen, this is Mark Cabaniss calling from Nashville, and although we've never met before…"

I kept talking for about fifteen seconds without taking a breath, hoping he wouldn't hang up. When I came up for air, he spoke in that trademark resonant baritone.

"I like that idea, Mark. Tell me more," he said.

Now I was on a roll. I told him about the Charles Kuralt/Loonis McGlohon program and that, thanks to Loonis, I now had a contact at NPR and I was eager to pitch this idea to them, but only if I could get Steve's commitment to be on board.

"Send me a first draft of the script, and I'll let you know my thoughts," he said.

I was thrilled! He didn't reject the idea out of hand. He was willing to give this stranger a shot. So I got to work that very night writing a script that would soon become *Steve Allen's Great American Songwriters*.

I researched all the composers to be featured, checked for availability of various recordings of their works I wanted to showcase, and then put the final touches on the script later that week. I overnighted it to Steve with my fingers crossed. Here was a man who'd written more than fifty books, and I figured he would be understandably particular.

About a week after I had sent him the script, my phone rang. It was Steve.

"Mark, this is Steve Allen. I'm calling about the script you sent to me."

I took a deep breath and saw my life flash before my eyes.

"Yes, yes," I responded, attempting to sound calm. "What do you think?"

"I think it's marvelous. You've really picked the best composers and their songs. Let's do it!" he said enthusiastically.

If this were a movie, I would freeze frame that moment right now of me on the phone, and the voice-over would say: "And he lived happily ever after."

To know that I was going to work with Steve Allen did make me very happy, and I couldn't wait to dig in! And I did just that in the weeks ahead. It involved three trips to Los Angeles, always to his impressive offices. The winding staircase that led up to his personal office was filled with framed magazine covers with Steve on them; posters of the films he'd been in or Broadway shows for which he'd written the music; and other memorabilia.

There was one question that burned in my mind to ask Steve before I met him. Here was a man who was known around the world for acting, composing, hosting, singing, dancing, writing, and more. He was awarded two stars on the Hollywood Walk of Fame, and a Hollywood theatre had been named in his honor. He had become one of the most universal entertainers of all time. Sir Noel Coward called him "The most talented man in America." Andy Williams once said, "Steve Allen does so many things, he's the only man I know who's listed on every one of the Yellow Pages."

And my burning question for Steve was…

"How did you do it?"

I wanted to know Steve's secret to success. Was it time management? Networking? Did he give up sleeping years ago? Just how did he become so ubiquitous?

But before I had that first meeting with him, I had answered my own question.

He did it because he could and because he had to. And that's to say nothing about his talent and intelligence that he obviously worked extremely hard to hone and paid the price to do so, year after year, decade after decade.

There's a line from the musical *The Fantasticks* that I've always loved. When the young ingénue Luisa asks the wise and seasoned narrator, El

Gallo, if she can climb a tree he's in to get a better perspective on things, he replies with five simple yet profound words:

"You can if you can."

Steve *could* and *did*.

Now that I had Steve fully committed to the project, the script approved, and NPR had accepted the concept and was ready to schedule the special in their lineup, only one minor detail remained to be solved. In my delirium of happiness, a thought struck me: *Where is the money coming from?*

Fortunately, Loonis had explained that important step of the process early on, and with my background in non-commercial broadcasting, I had been in a position before where I had to raise money for broadcast programming. But this was different. Steve Allen didn't come without a substantial and understandably high price tag, and there were several additional production expenses as well. This project would run into thousands and thousands of dollars. I was producing the program, and the job of raising the money always falls squarely in the producer's lap.

Raising money for these types of ventures—be it a broadcast program, a film, or a Broadway show—is very much a chicken-and-egg proposition. You can't get a network interested until you have a star on board, and you can't get a star on board until you have a network interested. And you can't get money until you have both. Sometimes you have to bluff on one side to get the other.

So I reached out once again to my best friend: the phone. And I started smiling and dialing. Not just anyone, of course, but the sources I knew who would be interested in having their names mentioned as sponsors over the airwaves, coast to coast. The good news was that I had a marquee star signed up and a major broadcast radio network on board. But getting people to part with money can be tricky, even when it's a worthy cause.

Finally, after about a month of networking and exploring options, I got there! The money was in the bank, and I gave NPR the green light to inform their member stations around the country that the curtain would rise on *Steve Allen's Great American Songwriters*. NPR had wisely suggested the show air on July Fourth, since the "great American" moniker seemed to fit with such a day.

What I then learned about NPR was that even though they would put the show on their satellite and could guarantee a certain number of their member stations would carry the show, a larger number of their stations could opt *not* to carry it. Since the show was a special, it wasn't required programming (unlike other NPR staples, such as *Morning Edition* or *All Things Considered*).

You mean to tell me I went through all of that to find that out?

Yep.

So what's a producer to do?

Promote, promote, promote, they said. Go to each station (via mail, phone, smoke signals, you name it) and pitch your show to them, encouraging them to carry it. Go sell 'em on it.

I told you earlier this wasn't going to be easy.

So once again, I got to work…this time writing letters, making phone calls, and stuffing envelopes with a demonstration recorded sample of the program to be mailed out to all the stations that might carry the show. And all of this was done at night or on weekends while I worked at my day job. But truthfully, I loved every minute of it.

During my meetings and conversations with Steve, I asked him what must have seemed like thousands of questions. But one topic we discussed was particularly fascinating: The King. Not official royalty. I'm talking about Elvis.

In 1956, NBC offered Allen a new, prime-time, Sunday night variety hour, the aforementioned Steve Allen Show, aimed at dethroning CBS's top-rated *Ed Sullivan Show*. The show included a typical run of star performers, including early TV appearances by Elvis Presley and Jerry Lee Lewis. Many popular film and television stars were guest stars, including Bob Hope, Doris Day, Kim Novak, Errol Flynn, Abbott and Costello, Esther Williams, Jerry Lewis, Martha Raye, the Three Stooges, and a host of others.

The show's regulars were Tom Poston, Louis Nye, Bill Dana, Don

Knotts, Pat Harrington Jr., Dayton Allen, and Gabriel Dell. All except film veteran Dell were relatively obscure performers prior to their stints with Allen, and all went on to stardom.

Although Steve was occasionally critical of some rock 'n' roll music in those days, he often booked rock 'n' roll acts on his show. I had read how Steve had famously scooped Ed Sullivan by being one of the first to present Elvis Presley on network television (after Presley had appeared on the Tommy and Jimmy Dorsey *Stage Show* and the *Milton Berle Show*, with a lot of controversy over his swiveling hips). But Steve found a way to satisfy the skeptics and get ratings gold.

"I assured viewers that I would not allow Presley to do anything that would offend anyone," Steve said. "NBC announced that a revamped, purified, and somewhat abridged Presley had agreed to sing while standing reasonably still, dressed in black tie." So Steve had Elvis wear a top hat and the white tie and tails of a high-class musician while singing "Hound Dog" to an actual hound, who was similarly attired. Outrageous!

"When I booked Elvis," he said, "I naturally had no interest in just presenting him vaudeville-style and letting him do his spot as he might in concert. Instead we worked him into the comedy fabric of our program. We certainly didn't inhibit Elvis's then notorious pelvic gyrations, but I think the fact that he had on formal evening attire made him, purely on his own, slightly alter his presentation."

With the Elvis appearance, Steve made television history once again.

"It was a hit," Steve said with a laugh. "Although afterwards, Elvis often called it the most ridiculous moment of his career, and he was probably right. But the viewers loved it."

You can see this historic and bizarre actual clip from the show on YouTube. Enter the words "Elvis hound dog Steve Allen," and there it will be.

The Steve Allen Show also featured plenty of jazz played by Steve and members of the show's band, which included flamboyantly comedic hipster trombonist Frank Rosolino (whom Steve credited with originating the "Hi-Ho!" chant later popularized by Ed McMahon on Johnny Carson's *Tonight Show*).

Another intriguing show of Steve's we discussed was his award-winning PBS series, *Meeting of the Minds*. From 1977 to 1981, Allen was the producer and host of this "talk show" with actors playing the parts of notable historical figures. The series pitted the likes of Socrates, Marie Antoinette, Thomas Paine, Sir Thomas More, Attila the Hun, Karl Marx, Emily Dickinson, Charles Darwin, and Galileo in dialog and argument. Steve's wife, the charismatic and elegant actress Jayne Meadows – a star in her own right – played a leading role in each program.

"I hope of all the things I did on television, I will be most remembered for that show," said Steve. "I believe that the issues and characters were timeless."

July Fourth, 1998, came literally with a bang…of fireworks that is. And according to NPR, *Steve Allen's Great American Songwriters* hit with a bang as well…achieving eighty-eight percent coverage of all NPR member stations, making it one of their most successful specials that year! At my request, Steve had recorded a string of promotional spots for each respective city where the show was to be aired prior to the air date. Those promotions helped immensely in building anticipation and listenership for the show. Being the trouper he was, Steve didn't bat an eye as he recorded dozens of promotional spots inviting listeners from Dubuque to Denver to tune in. Accordingly, the show was heard by millions. NPR, the member stations, the sponsors, and Steve were all very happy. And needless to say, so was I. Another one of my "what-if" moments had become a dream come true.

In addition to a warm and congratulatory phone call from Steve the day after the show aired, I received a letter from him, which is framed and hangs in my office to this day. Truly a memory that will live on forever for me. Working with "the most talented man in America" proved to be one of my proudest moments as a producer.

A few years after my work with Steve, on October 30, 2000, he was driving to the home of his son (Bill, who told me he was a big fan of *Steve Allen's Great American Songwriters*) in Encino, California, when his car was struck by another vehicle backing out of a driveway. Neither Steve nor the other driver believed he was injured, and damage to both vehicles was minimal, so the two exchanged insurance information and Allen continued on his way.

Shortly after arriving at his son's home, Steve did not feel well and excused himself. After a while, Bill became concerned and entered the room to find Steve motionless. Paramedics were summoned but could not revive him. The postmortem revealed that he had not suffered major injuries from the car accident, but the cause of death was a massive heart attack caused by a ruptured artery. Allen's personal physician believed it had been triggered by shock due to the collision, which was aggravated by his age and preexisting coronary artery disease.

The genius of Steve Allen had been silenced at the age of seventy-eight. But he had remained very active right until the end. Just as he wanted it, I'm sure.

Entire books have been written about Steve, so this chapter is an embarrassingly brief and clumsy attempt to capture the essence of this multifaceted, brilliant, witty, and warm human being.

I am honored to have known and worked with Steve Allen. His humanity and amazing career will always serve as a source of fascination and inspiration to me.

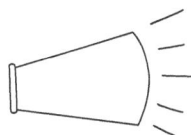

WAIT, WAIT... THERE'S MORE!

You can visit the official Steve Allen website: www.steveallen.com to learn more about this entertainment icon.

THE GAME OF WORD

Word Records started out with a fascinating and somewhat accidental, if not providential, beginning back in 1951. Jarrell McCracken was its founder. (Side note: Although I never had the pleasure of meeting McCracken, one of the choral anthems I'd written years before titled "Celtic Prayer" was sung by a choir at his funeral. I was honored.)

Word Records' name is based on a sixteen-minute spoken word recording written and narrated by McCracken, the first recording released by the label, titled the "The Game of Life." The twenty-three-year-old KWTX sportscaster in Waco had read an article by Jimmy Allen, a former athlete who became a Baptist preacher, and based his recording on the article, which also is called "The Game of Life." The event is based on a full-length match between the forces of Good and Evil with Jesus and Satan coaching the two teams. McCracken was familiar with play-by-play broadcasting, having created virtual baseball games for radio broadcast based on wire reports. McCracken originally presented his "Game of Life" on Sunday nights at various churches around the central Texas area. Everywhere he presented "The Game of Life," he got requests for copies. Eventually, he had a short run of records pressed to offer at churches where he spoke. The fictional radio station in the recording has the call letters "WORD" so that was printed on the label of the custom record. After being asked by a friend when he was going to release a follow-up, McCracken decided to pursue the label on a more serious level. The rest is gospel music history.

Word has since had a checkered past with the usual (some would say more than usual) ups and downs of a record label. In 1976, McCracken sold a large portion of it to ABC-TV, then to what became ABC/Capital Cities (at which time the company forced McCracken out). It has since changed hands several additional times…from ABC/Cap Cities to Thomas Nelson, then to Gaylord Entertainment, then to AOL/Time Warner, then to Warner Music Group (as of this writing).

I'd had several business interactions with Word through the years. During my time at Hal Leonard, I reached out to Don Cason while he was head of Word's print music division to see if he might be open to a distribution deal between Word and Hal Leonard. This ended up creating what became a very lucrative deal for both Word and Hal Leonard.

Similarly, when I'd gone to Shawnee Press, I reached out to Word to see if they would distribute to the Christian retail trade the new Shawnee Press songbooks I was going to create. Word accepted my proposal, and that, too, became a profitable deal for Word and Shawnee.

So I had gotten to know the folks at Word pretty well over the years. Accordingly, I had come to know the company well enough to sense the volatile nature of it and the record business – which would become all the more volatile in the 2000s as the record business changed radically with the onset of illegal downloading on the Internet.

Mark Funderburg, then president of Word Distribution, asked me out to lunch one day. I knew and liked Mark, but we'd never had lunch before so I wasn't sure what might be on his mind. About halfway through the entrée, he played his cards.

"Mark, would you consider leaving Shawnee Press and joining Word to head up our print music division?"

I didn't see that coming. I told Mark that while I was flattered, I didn't have any desire to move to another company then, but if that ever changed,

I would let him know. (This meeting, as noted before, took place about two months before my meeting with Barrie Edwards in Santa Monica.)

As I drove away from my meeting with Mark Funderburg, I thought of another Mark. I'd heard Mark Bright, then president/CEO of Word, was under pressure from Word's current owner, Warner Music Group, to hire someone to head up their print division and get it back to its glory days. Or at least turn around the substantial slide in revenues it had been experiencing over the last decade. As I mentioned earlier, Word had been without a leader for more than a year, and the strain was starting to show (it was like déjà vu with Shawnee Press having been leaderless before I was called in to tighten things up).

Soon after my meeting with Mark Funderburg, I was attending the annual CMPA (Church Music Publishers Association) convention. Mark Bright was also attending and asked me to join him for dinner, which proceeded to be a three-hour *tête-à-tête*, when he discussed with me the idea of joining Word to head up Word Music, their print music division.

Despite Mark's wooing, I was very reluctant to join Word. It wasn't that I didn't like the people I'd met at Word. I did. There were (and are) several wonderful, talented, and passionate people at Word. It's just that I knew I didn't want to jump in the middle of what everyone on the outside (and inside) knew to be a volatile and ever-changing situation. Don Cason, a twenty-eight-year veteran of Word, and David Guthrie, another veteran of Word, had been given pink slips after long tenures there because of a decade of declining sales (due to the shifting and shrinking evangelical print music business). Since Don's and David's painful departures, the remaining staff was trying to hold things together, but (according to Word management at the time as they described the situation to me), they were a "ship without a captain or direction." Plus, due to Word's being bought and sold so many times over the years (with dozens of employees losing jobs), there always seemed to be a feeling of malaise and snarky attitude that hovered over the building…sort of a "Who's next?" mentality.

Then later, with the collapse of the possibility of my buying Shawnee

Press, if I didn't want to conduct a full-on job search in an industry that was continuing to change rapidly, I needed to accept the job offer from Word. So true to my word to Reiff Lorenz that day in Dayton, I took the job at Word.

In May 2009, I met with Mark Bright in a recording studio on Music Row, where he was working on the newest Carrie Underwood record. I told him I'd decided to accept the position. He was delighted and hugged me. I walked away, relieved I'd made the final decision and would soon be starting what I knew would be a very challenging job (to say the least).

I was very appreciative to have a place to go and continue my work in the music business. But it didn't ultimately feel as if it was a good fit from Day One for several reasons. Nevertheless, I threw myself into it wholeheartedly.

And the pressure was on…non-stop at a level I'd never experienced in my twenty years in the music business. When there's a billion-dollar parent company looking over your shoulder, that parent is like a "beast that hungers," and the beast must be fed. Regardless of market trends. Despite the pressure, the team I put into place pulled together, rolled up their sleeves and we made some wonderful and unprecedented successes happen.

Word's (then) parent company, Warner Music Group, had gotten out of the print music business in 2005 (yes…the aforementioned print music effort called Warner Brothers Publications they had started years before to compete with Shawnee Press had finally run its course, and they had sold it to Alfred Music, the world's largest educational music publisher based in Los Angeles. An educational music publisher focuses on music for school, church, and home – like a Shawnee Press or Hal Leonard). After Warner got out of the print music business, I (along with many others in the print music biz) was a bit puzzled why Warner had retained the Word Music print division of Word Entertainment. Warner is a record company (with Warner-Chappell publishing attached – which is not a print music company), and record companies don't understand (or really care about) print. Never have. Never will. Nor should they. It's just not what they do (and vice versa for print companies regarding the record business). To me, a record company being in the print business is like a three-hundred-pound football linebacker trying to be a ballet dancer. I suppose it can be done, but it is going to be awkward and extremely difficult. And not always pretty.

One former Word Music employee was absolutely stunned when he asked and I told him I had a staff of four (excluding my seven-member sales team). "We did less amount of product that you're putting out, and we had fifteen people" (again, excluding the sales team). So I was producing more product than was being produced in years prior with a staff roughly a fourth the size. It was an absolute zoo, and I was growing increasingly weary of the job and sympathetic to those four souls who were stretched way, way beyond their limits. Something had to give. And it did.

It was soon announced that Universal Music (by now the owner of Brentwood-Benson Music Publishing) and EMI were to merge. Those of us who paid attention to the print world knew that meant one of two things: Either Dale Mathews (my former boss from my Brentwood Music days who was now president of Brentwood-Benson) would be out of a job, or Eddie DeGarmo (president of EMI Christian Music Publishing) would be out of a job. The newly created entity probably wouldn't need both of them.

I was in Florida to speak at a music event when I saw an e-mail on my phone that had come from "Capitol CMG Publishing." I found out this was what the newly merged Universal/Brentwood-Benson/EMI Christian Publishing entity was now called. I opened the e-mail immediately and read it with great interest.

I kept scrolling down to see what would become of Dale or Eddie. And there it was: Dale would be leaving Brentwood-Benson after twenty-seven years to "pursue other interests."

I immediately called my director of sales and marketing at Word to discuss this change with him. I knew this shift would have far-reaching ramifications for our industry.

For the next few weeks, things were status quo at Word, but then I got wind confidentially that the idea was being floated of doing a similar cost-cutting measure at Word that had been executed on Dale Mathews by Capitol CMG. The scuttle I was getting was that Word/Warner wanted to combine print and publishing at Word into one position (thus eliminating my position along with Word's head of publishing position) and hire Dale (who was now suddenly available) to do both.

And now, we pause the action to rewind yet again to a few years before this all came down (as Professor Harold Hill says to Shirley Jones as Marian the Librarian in act 2 of *The Music Man*, "There's never a peaceful moment in the music business." How true, Professor, how true).

I'd become dear friends with the legendary Morty and Iris Manus, the husband-wife patriarch and matriarch of the aforementioned Alfred Music. Of all the people I've met in the music business over the years, Morty and Iris had fast become two of my all-time favorite people, not only in the music business but in life. Here were two kind, generous, talented, interesting, intelligent, and extremely successful people. They had worked very hard for the success of Alfred Music (a company in business for more than ninety years), and their work had paid off. Alfred remained a major force through the ups and downs of the very difficult music business.

When I was at lunch in Manhattan with Morty and Iris, Morty said to me that he and Iris would like Alfred to get back in the church music business someday (Alfred had stepped back from that segment of the business for a while). And Morty said they would like me to help Alfred do that.

I had been acquainted with Alfred since I was in grade school. Alfred was considered an "Educational Music Publisher" meaning they focused on educational music for schools primarily. I'd written my master's thesis on an educational music publisher (Hinshaw Music), and had a bachelor's degree in music education, so after my experience with Hal Leonard and Shawnee Press (both educational music publishers), the prospect of joining Alfred felt like going home.

I was flattered and honored. I told him that I'd always wanted to own my own music publisher, and might I make a run at purchasing their church catalog?

Accordingly, I was once again in my (then) attorney's office (Kurt Beasley) four years after my first period with him discussing my desire to try to buy Shawnee Press. He was interested in helping as he had during the Shawnee proposal, and we started our due diligence. This time, however, I brought in Tom Bogan, former Brentwood-Benson CFO (who also had thirty years of experience in the music business with a heavy concentration on acquisitions). Tom, Kurt, and I hunkered down to do the numbers regarding Alfred's church business.

But the second time was not the charm. After careful due diligence, we made an offer to Alfred for the catalog but were too far apart in our respective valuations. We parted amicably. But I had set the stage to learn even more this time (as I did previously with the failed Shawnee Press acquisition) about what it takes to buy a music publisher (it ain't easy).

The changes at Word eventually happened several weeks later: The print division and publishing divisions at Word were combined; Dale Mathews went to Word to head up print and publishing, and Chad Segura (the head of Word Publishing) and I were out. This was a business move, and business is business. Frankly, it made sense. It was a money-saving move at the very least.

Fortunately, however, before the changes happened at Word, thanks to Morty and Iris Manus, the wheels had already started turning for my next adventure in the music business. I believe there are no accidents and God closes doors to open new windows.

A few years after Dale Mathews went to Word, Warner Music Group had finally had a belly full of the Gospel music business and put Word Entertainment (including Word Music, the print division) on the block for sale. The venerable Mike Curb (who had owned 20% of Word Entertainment for years) stepped in to purchase the 80% of Word Entertainment that Warner was unloading. But Curb didn't want the print division. So Word Music was also shopped and then purchased by Lorenz Corporation. Lorenz scratched a decades long-held itch to jump into the evangelical print industry whole hog. But when Covid hit a few years after Lorenz purchased Word, and sales completely tanked across the board for all print music publishers in an unprecedented fashion, Lorenz evidently couldn't keep their promises to the bank for the loan they floated to buy Word and had to declare bankruptcy. It was ugly in many ways: Word Music shuttered, all employees were fired (including Dale), operations (what remained) of Word Music moved to Lorenz's Dayton, Ohio headquarters, and product development came to a screeching halt. Lorenz soon had to sell its 100+ year old building and printing presses and greatly reduce staff. Years later as of this writing, only a tiny number of products trickle out of Word each year. A sad turn of events for a once powerhouse publisher. It may rise from the ashes yet. Who knows.

DICK CLARK'S ROCKIN' CAREER

Here's another example of an American icon who is no longer with us, and for those readers unfamiliar with him, I encourage you to read on.

Steve Allen knew Dick Clark well, and Dick had referred to Steve as a "hero." So while I was working with Steve, I asked him if he would set up a meeting with Dick and me, at least by phone. Steve happily obliged. Dick was another person who had fascinated and inspired me through the years. I was interested in possibly following up the success of the Steve Allen NPR special I'd produced with something hosted by Dick Clark. NPR loved the idea.

The difficulty of getting a meeting with Dick Clark was the stuff of urban legend. An entire sketch on NBC-TV's *Saturday Night Live* was created around the premise that no one…not even the Messiah Himself…had easy access to Dick Clark.

Dick Clark was an American radio and television personality, as well as a cultural icon who remains best known for hosting American television's longest-running variety show, *American Bandstand,* from 1957 to 1987. The show's popularity also helped Dick become an American media mogul and inspired similar long-running music programs, such as *Soul Train* and *Top of the Pops.*

He also hosted the game show *The $25,000 Pyramid* and *TV's Bloopers* *and Practical Jokes* (with Ed McMahon). For thirty years *Dick Clark's New Year's Rockin' Eve* transmitted Times Square's New Year's Eve celebrations worldwide (the program continues on ABC-TV as *New Year's Rockin' Eve* with host Ryan Seacrest). Clark was also well known for his trademark sign-off, "For now, Dick Clark. So long!" accompanied with a military salute.

As host of *American Bandstand*, Clark introduced rock and roll to many Americans. The show gave many new music artists their first exposure to national audiences, including Ike and Tina Turner, Smokey Robinson and the Miracles, Stevie Wonder, Talking Heads, and Simon & Garfunkel. Episodes he hosted were among the first where blacks and whites performed on the same stage and among the first where the live studio audience sat without racial segregation. Singer Paul Anka claimed that *Bandstand* was responsible for creating a "youth culture."

In his capacity as a businessman, Clark served as chief executive officer of Dick Clark Productions, part of which he sold off in his later years. He also founded the *American Bandstand* Diner, a restaurant chain modeled after the Hard Rock Cafe. In 1973, he created and produced the annual *American Music Awards* show, designed to compete with the Grammy Awards when ABC-TV's contract to broadcast the Grammys expired.

My phone rang one summer afternoon, and it was Steve Allen's assistant, Daryl, who had the good news to report that he had spoken with Dick Clark's assistant and Dick was willing to chat with me about my idea. Daryl gave me Dick's phone number, and I immediately called it to set up my chat with "America's Oldest Teenager" (as he was often referred to because of his perennial youthful appearance).

The phone call took place the next day and lasted about thirty minutes. But those were thirty fascinating and unforgettable minutes.

"Hi, Mr. Clark," I said, trying to catch my breath as I spoke to yet another one of my heroes.

"Thanks for the call, Mark. Steve Allen told me you were going to share an idea with me," he said in that trademark voice. "And you can call me Dick."

I told him my idea of a radio special I wanted to produce titled *Dick Clark's Century of Song*...featuring some of the great songs of the last century.

"I like that idea. However, we've got a project here at my company that's actually similar to that concept we're working on right now. But since yours is for radio and ours is for television, they might co-exist just fine together," he said.

We chatted more about the concept and approach, and he asked me to send him a show outline and he would share it with his team for consideration. He liked the idea of doing radio again for a one-time special. Before we wrapped things up, I couldn't help but ask a few questions about his illustrious and monumental career. What about *American Bandstand*?

"*Bandstand* was a hit maker," he said enthusiastically. "Once a song was heard on the show, radio disc jockeys and program directors coast to coast would hear the song and say, 'Hey, we'd better start playing that song.' Sheet music and record sales followed."

And what were his thoughts about doing the New Year's broadcast for so many years?

"It's very nice to be welcomed into people's celebrations, whether it's a party or bar mitzvah or Christmas or New Year's. I consider it an honor and have enjoyed it very much over the years."

Any stories about the "live" element of the broadcast?

"Live television is always exhilarating. We're spoiled these days with taping and the luxury of retake after retake. If you fall on your face during live TV, you just have to get up and keep going. That's not only a great professional lesson to be learned but a life lesson. If you fall down, get up and walk again. If you can't walk, crawl. If one idea fails, have another one. I have failed a lot in my life, but I always have the next thing planned. Success doesn't happen by accident. It takes a lot of hard work."

I didn't want to keep him any longer. I considered myself extremely fortunate to have any time with this very busy legend. But I had to ask him one final question.

"Dick, you've been so successful in your multifaceted career. What do you enjoy most about it?" I asked.

He paused a moment and then spoke reflectively.

"I've always worked in light entertainment, and I'm not ashamed of that. There's so much heaviness in the world somebody's gotta be the class clown, to give you a laugh. If I take people away from their problems and give them an escape, that's good.

"I'm the luckiest man you'll ever meet. I've done what I love doing for my entire career. It doesn't get any better than that."

Dick Clark suffered a stroke in December 2004. With his speech ability still impaired, he returned to his *New Year's Rockin' Eve* show a year later on December 31, 2005. Subsequently, he appeared at the 58th Primetime Emmy Awards in 2006, and every *New Year's Rockin' Eve* show through the 2011–2012 shows. Clark died on April 18, 2012, of a heart attack at age eighty-two following a medical procedure.

Because of his stroke, we were never able to pursue the idea of us working together on a radio special together. But I'll always be thankful to have spent a few minutes with someone who inspired me then and continues to inspire me now, and who was as nice privately as he seemingly was publicly.

OZ, JAZZ, AND JUDY

The only person in the world who could bring Oz (as in The Land of), jazz, and Judy (Garland, that is) – among other things and people – together was an unforgettable man with an unforgettable name: Loonis.

Loonis McGlohon was unforgettable not only because he was tremendously talented as a jazz pianist (he had his own Loonis McGlohon Trio), composer, broadcaster, and producer but also because he was a true southern raconteur.

Born in Ayden, North Carolina, Loonis graduated from East Carolina University. After a stint in the Air Force during World War II, he played piano with the Jimmy Dorsey and Jack Teagarden Orchestras. Loonis was one of North Carolina's earliest broadcasters at the state's first television station in Charlotte, serving as music director for WBT (AM) radio and WBTV (Charlotte's CBS-TV affiliate).

I had grown up watching Loonis on WBTV and was fascinated by his ability to blend broadcasting and music (there's that theme again!). I often saw Loonis appear on WBTV with his easygoing, southern charm. He also loved another one of my passions: *American Popular Song* (think Cole Porter, George and Ira Gershwin, Hoagy Carmichael, and others from that era). Toward that end, he was co-host of the Peabody

Award-winning NPR radio series *American Popular Song* with his friend and collaborator, Alec Wilder (for those readers unfamiliar with Alec Wilder, do a Google search and you'll be amazed at the work of this eccentric genius).

So once upon a time on a Tuesday morning in Nashville, I decided, "I want to work with Loonis McGlohon." So I picked up my best friend (the phone) once again and got to work on making it happen.

My first call, naturally, was to WBTV, and after a few conversations explaining I was in the music publishing business and wanted to work with Loonis, I got his phone number. My next call was to Loonis himself. He answered.

"Mr. McGlohon, you don't know me, but I've watched you for years on WBTV...," and on my pitch went.

"First of all, you must call me Loonis. And secondly, what did you say your name was? You haven't taken a breath yet," he said with a chuckle.

I hadn't breathed because I was speaking to one of my heroes! Our conversation lasted for about thirty minutes, and it was like speaking with a friend I'd known for years. I was to be in North Carolina a few weeks later, and we arranged to have dinner.

In the years that passed, whenever I flew into Charlotte on a business or personal trip, Loonis picked me up at the airport. I then spent the night with him and his wife, Nan, at their wonderful, welcoming home. Each trip featured dining at Charlotte's finest restaurants, and a string of Charlotte's most prominent citizens always happened by, wanting to chat with the couple. Breakfast the next morning was at the McGlohon kitchen table, and I never knew who would drop by. Loonis had a coterie of musicians, actors, broadcasters, and producers who circled him at any given moment...all fascinating people with their own stories to tell.

What I found out soon after meeting Loonis was that he'd been battling lymphoma for about a year, and it had taken a toll on him. But he was a fighter, and Nan said the writing assignments I gave him were "giving him a good reason to write music again." Amazingly, he had pretty much maintained a busy performance and producing schedule throughout his cancer treatment.

Shawnee Press had published several of his sacred songs, and in addition to his busy broadcast and performing schedule through the years, he'd managed to make time to be a part-time choir director at Carmel Presbyterian in Charlotte. So sacred music was yet another passion we shared. During our professional and personal friendship, we eventually created three CD recordings of our favorite hymns and gospel songs (he played piano; I produced), and they sold coast to coast (and are still available to this day).

Legendary singers including Judy Garland, Mabel Mercer, and Eileen Farrell were accompanied at the piano by Loonis. Among the songs he wrote with Alec Wilder are "Blackberry Winter," "Be a Child," and "While We're Young." Loonis, like Wilder, could write both music and lyrics, and for his hit "Songbird" he wrote both.

In 1980, Frank Sinatra recorded two of his songs written with Alec—"South to a Warmer Place" and "A Long Night."

Loonis had a lot of great stories, and everyone always enjoyed the one about the legendary Judy Garland. "As you can imagine, Judy was like no one else you'd ever met in your life. She was impulsive, funny, impossible, and wonderful," Loonis said, with a smile on his face, looking as if he'd just seen her yesterday.

"I'll never forget when I was her pianist for a series of concerts at a cabaret setting in London. She was nearing the end of her career but still had that remarkable talent and passion for singing and performing.

"Near the end of the concert, she looked at me and said, 'Loonis, this is a special audience.' That, of course, was followed by applause. And then she said, 'So I want to do something special for them. Will you play it for me?'

"I then launched into the introduction to 'Over the Rainbow,' and the applause was thunderous. She then sang it with all the heart and passion you can imagine, and with the way her life had turned out, everyone felt the poignancy of this legendary and battered star whom we'd seen as a child and genuinely seemed to want to go over the rainbow to escape her troubles.

By the end of the song, tears were streaming down her cheeks, and the audience was transfixed as I've never seen an audience before. There wasn't a dry eye in the house. After she finished the song and took her bows, the applause shook the rafters."

And then he added the kicker: "We did two shows a night for six nights, and she said and did *the same thing at every single show.*"

Proof positive that Judy Garland was an entertainer who understood show business and knew how to make an audience feel special and give them what they came for. And then some.

Another one of Loonis's most famous friends was CBS-TV broadcaster Charles Kuralt. Charles was also a noted North Carolinian, and together, Loonis and Charles were commissioned to write a tribute to North Carolina in celebration of the state's 400th birthday. The result was a forty-minute work for orchestra, narrator, and soloists titled *North Carolina Is My Home*. It started out as a recording, then became a live concert event (with Kuralt narrating and Loonis playing piano) and eventually was produced as a public television special and even a coffee table book.

I remember the night when I flew to Charlotte to see what would be the final time Loonis and Charles ever presented *North Carolina Is My Home*. There, in a beautifully refurbished theatre (renamed The McGlohon Theatre by Loonis's good friend, Hugh McColl, then CEO of Bank of America… yet another shameless name-drop for you), I saw Loonis and Charles perform this "Valentine for North Carolina" to great acclaim. Afterward, I was invited to an intimate gathering of North Carolina's inner circle, which included then North Carolina Governor Jim Hunt. But Loonis and Nan spoke to them and introduced me to everyone as if we were sitting at their kitchen table. Never an ounce of pretense was present in them…whether they were entertaining North Carolina's finest at a fancy home or talking to a ticket taker at the movie theatre, they were down to earth and real.

Another example of Loonis's personal touch occurred when he was invited to appear at a major fund-raising event at a private club in my hometown. He had told me he was going to perform there, and since I was far away in Nashville and couldn't attend, he asked if my parents (who still lived there at the time) would like to be his invited guests at the event. "Absolutely…I'm sure they would be delighted to come," I said.

When my parents walked into the room that night, while many were happy to see them, a few of the more snooty eyebrows were raised that my parents seemed to be crashing the party. "Just who do they think they are?" a few of them mumbled. The minute Loonis saw my parents sitting in the back of the room, he immediately ushered them to front-row seats next to him, all to the stunned amazement of those haughty guests. Loonis relished the opportunity to showcase my parents, who were just happy to be there (and were probably the wisest and nicest people in the room).

Although my first "live" connection with Loonis was on the phone that first day, in addition to his work on WBTV, I was familiar with his work through another major and very unique project he wrote (also with Alec Wilder). That project was the music score for The Land of Oz, an outdoor theme park in the mountains of Western North Carolina.

The Land of Oz (now defunct) was located in the resort town of Beech Mountain. It was opened in 1970 by Grover Robbins, who had been successful with Tweetsie Railroad (a long-time independent North Carolina theme park) and was fully operational until 1980. Visitors could take a walk down the Yellow Brick Road, "experience" the cyclone that struck Dorothy's house, and visit with the Scarecrow, the Tin Woodman, the Cowardly Lion, and the Wicked Witch of the West. The Yellow Brick Road led to a show at the Emerald City where the characters met with the Wizard. An artificial balloon ride (a specially modified ski lift) allowed visitors to get a bird's-eye view of the park and mountain scenery before leaving Oz. A small museum showcased props and costumes from the film. These were jointly bought by the park and Debbie Reynolds from MGM.

The complete journey through Oz was accompanied with music by Loonis and Alec, and the score was delightful. As a child going to the park, I was enthralled by the entire process, and the name Loonis McGlohon caught my attention, even as a nine-year old.

Years later, I was visiting Loonis and Nan one weekend at their second home in Beech Mountain (which they had obtained as a part of his deal for writing the score for Land of Oz). Knowing that I had a special place in my heart for his work on the Oz score, Loonis said to me at breakfast he wanted to take me somewhere up the road and show me a special place.

We drove for about five minutes up and down some winding mountain roads, then arrived at a clearing. We got out of the car, and he led me up to the Yellow Brick Road! It was still intact after all these years, even if the theme park was not. Several of the trees still had the sculpted faces on them and the witch's castle and lion's den were still there, along with Dorothy's house. As we walked down that iconic Yellow Brick Road, he reminisced about writing the score for what became North Carolina's most popular tourist attraction in its day.

When we got back to his home, he said he had a gift for me. He excused himself and then came out with a yellow brick…from the Land of Oz's Yellow Brick Road. The owners of the theme park had given Loonis six of them – pulled directly from the road when the park closed – as mementos to Loonis. He'd given out all as gifts, except one. He'd had it for years.

"This brick is for you, Mark. You probably walked on it as a nine-year-old child when you came to Oz. I'd been saving this brick for someone special, and I decided that someone is you. I hope you'll always remember that just like it was a dream of mine to work with Alec Wilder – and that dream came true – you have dreams too. And like the song 'Over the Rainbow' says, 'Dreams really do come true.'"

Working with and getting to know Loonis McGlohon were truly a dream come true for me. He succumbed to cancer one year later in January 2002. The Oz brick sits in my home in Nashville with a small brass-engraved plate attached to it, which commemorates this special gift. Every time I see it, I'm reminded of my dear friend, the talented and amazing Loonis McGlohon, who inspires me to this day.

I KISSED A GHOST

The road to meeting a ghost began with Hoagy Carmichael.

Well, not *the* Hoagy—he had long since taken his seat in that great Stardust Supper Club in the sky—but with his songs (and his son, Hoagy Bix Carmichael).

Thanks to some timely help from my friend Kevin Lamb (then the managing executive at Peermusic Nashville), I managed to acquire the non-exclusive stage rights to the Carmichael catalog. With those in hand, I teamed up with Alan Bailey, the Georgia-born co-writer of the Off-Broadway hit *Smoke on the Mountain*, to create a jukebox musical built around Hoagy's unforgettable tunes.

Hoagy Carmichael, one of America's most beloved songwriters, left us with an unmatched legacy of standards that still shimmer today. His catalog includes the hauntingly beautiful "Stardust," the wistful "Skylark" (with lyrics by Johnny Mercer), the playful Oscar-winning "In the Cool, Cool, Cool of the Evening," the tender duet "Two Sleepy People," and, of course, the immortal "Georgia on My Mind." These songs not only defined an era but continue to find fresh life in every new generation of singers.

I named the musical *The Stardust Supper Club*—a funny and heartfelt show set in a little Indiana nightclub on the night of the 1952 Academy Awards broadcast. Through a cast of five, Hoagy's music became the soundtrack for small-town dreams, jealousies, reconciliations, and romance. After months of writing and re-writing, we finally gathered Broadway pros for a table read and music rehearsal in Los Angeles at none other than Debbie Reynolds' rehearsal studios. (Only in show business can you casually say, "We'll be at Debbie Reynolds' place.") Our cast that day included Marc Kudisch and Leslie Margherita—both Broadway powerhouse performers who made our little workshop sing.

Next came the "up on its feet" stage: a proper workshop production with blocking, costumes, and an audience. For that, we turned to Off-Broadway's York Theatre in New York City. And what a cast we assembled: Broadway treasures Carolee Carmello and Jason Graae in the leads. Pros through and through, they brought nuance and heart to every scene.

Moments before curtain, Alan leaned over to me and whispered, "By the way, my friend Marni Nixon is in the audience tonight."

I froze. "*The* Marni Nixon?" I asked. (As if there were dozens of them roaming around Manhattan.)

"Yes," Alan replied. "That's the one!"

"Marni who?" you reader dear may ask. And I reply: You know her voice (even if you don't know her name).

Marni Nixon was Hollywood's most famous *"ghost singer."*

- Deborah Kerr's elegant vocals in *The King and I*? That was Marni.
- Natalie Wood's belting and lyrical singing in *West Side Story*? Still Marni.
- Audrey Hepburn's "I Could Have Danced All Night" (and all the other songs for Eliza Doolittle in *My Fair Lady*?) Yep—Marni again.

For years, audiences swooned without ever knowing whose voice they were hearing. While the stars mouthed the words on screen, Marni was the one making the magic in the recording studio.

Marni wasn't just a hidden talent, though. She was one of the nuns

(Sister Sophia) in the immortal Robert Wise film *The Sound of Music* (with Julie Andrews, of course). Marni's the one who joins in the song "How do you solve a problem like Maria?" along with Sisters Berthe and Margaretta.

And the ironic thing about her connection with Julie Andrews: After originating the role of Eliza Doolittle on the Broadway stage in what became an acclaimed performance, Julie was famously and heartbreakingly passed over for the role of Eliza in the film version for box office bonanza Audrey Hepburn. And although Audrey tried valiantly to sing the role on screen, her voice was ultimately deemed insufficient to meet the vocal demands of the role, and Marni was brought in to dub it.

Marni also had a busy concert and teaching career, and even wrote her memoir *I Could Have Sung All Night*.

In short: if you've ever loved a classic Hollywood musical, chances are you've already "met" Marni Nixon—you just didn't know it.

I had played Alfred Doolittle in our high school production of *My Fair Lady*, and that experience and show became very dear (and transformative in some ways) to and for me. And I learned the show before auditions by listening to—again and again and again—the film soundtrack . . . and Marni (even though as a high school student, I didn't know about Hollywood dubbing yet). Bottom line: I knew I couldn't let the evening go by without at least saying hello to this legend (especially one so deeply connected to my beloved *My Fair Lady*).

So before the show began, I walked out into the audience and spotted her immediately—sitting elegantly in a February scarf that somehow managed to look both warm and glamorous.

I introduced myself: "Ms. Nixon, I'm Mark Cabaniss, the co-writer of tonight's show. Thank you so much for being here."

She smiled warmly. "Mark, it's my pleasure. Alan has told me a lot about the show, and it sounds delightful. We're excited to see it. And please call me Marni."

I told her what an enormous fan I was, how I had read her book, and how her career had inspired me and so many others. She graciously accepted the compliments with a twinkle in her eye. "Thank you for those beautiful and kind words, Mark. I've been very fortunate to do what I do all these years."

We continued to chat a few more minutes about what she was up to those days, and her love for film and the theatre. I was in Heaven. And she was (not surprisingly) very gracious and charming.

As showtime drew near, I leaned down to give her a light hug. And then, to my astonishment, she kissed me on the cheek. I instinctively returned the gesture.

And that's how I kissed a ghost.

The York performance went beautifully that night, playing to a full house. Among those in attendance was Hoagy Bix Carmichael, who later created his own stage show of his father's music (but that's another story).

Still, the moment I'll always treasure most from that night wasn't in the script. It was that gracious, unforgettable encounter with the legendary Marni Nixon. She may have been Hollywood's most famous "ghost singer," but she certainly didn't ghost me that night.

A MAN FOR ALL SEASONS

Don't be late for the plane...don't be late for the plane.

That admonition rolled over in my mind several times with as much conviction as if delivered by a motivational speaker. I was being tempted to make a quick side trip to the nearby Barnes and Noble bookstore as I drove to the airport. I had heard of a new best-selling book that I thought would be good reading during the flight. *Oh, what the heck*, I thought. *I'll drive a little faster.* I was flying to Los Angeles, so I needed something good to help fill the several hours I would spend on the plane. So I hurried into the bookstore even as I envisioned chasing the plane down the runway as it lifted off. (Have you ever had *that* dream before? Hmmm...dreams. That's another fascinating discussion for another book. But I digress.)

As I rushed into the store, I noticed a poster in the shop window that promoted an upcoming personal appearance at the store from – none other than – Rupert Holmes. He would be there the following Thursday evening to sign copies of his new novel, *Where the Truth Lies* (which would later be made into a motion picture starring Colin Firth and Kevin Bacon). Fortunately, I would be back home by Thursday. By all means, I had to be there!

Like millions of others, I had first become acquainted with Rupert Holmes through his pop hits. Not only was he the writer of those hits; he was the singer. Among his many Billboard-charting smashes were "Escape (The Pina Colada Song)" – which reached number one on the Billboard charts—and "Him" (which reached number six). Other favorites of mine included "Answering Machine," "Widescreen," and "Echo Valley 2-6809" (recorded by David Cassidy and heard on TV's *The Partridge Family*). But those are only the tip of the iceberg for this prolific writer.

In 1971, Rupert had his first international Top-40 hit, "Timothy." Holmes also wrote jingles and pop tunes for others, including Gene Pitney, the Platters, the Drifters, Wayne Newton, Dolly Parton, and Barry Manilow.

As a recording artist, Holmes broke through with his first album, 1974's Widescreen, on Epic Records, which introduced him as a presenter of highly romantic, lushly orchestrated "story songs" that told a witty narrative punctuated by clever rhymes and a hint of comedy. Barbra Streisand discovered this album and asked to record songs from it, launching Holmes on a successful career. She then used some of his songs in the movie *A Star Is Born*. He also arranged, conducted, and wrote songs on her 1975 album, *Lazy Afternoon*, and five of her other albums. Holmes's second, self-titled album led *Rolling Stone* to compare him with Bob Dylan in the sense of being an artist of unprecedented originality who commanded attention.

Rupert has had praise heaped on him from numerous industry legends and others from around the world. From Rita Coolidge to Barry Manilow to *The New York Times* and *The Los Angeles Times*—he has been called a "genius" and "national treasure." Those are well-deserved and accurate descriptions of this true *Renaissance man*.

"In addition" are the two words that must be used again and again when describing Rupert's career. So, in addition to everything else, Rupert created and wrote the critically hailed, Emmy Award—winning comedy/drama television series *Remember WENN* for the American Movie Classics network. Set at the fictional Pittsburgh radio station WENN in the early 1940s, it depicted events in the personal and professional lives of the station's staff in the era before and during World War II. Holmes also composed the show's theme, its songs, and its poignant underscore over the course of its four seasons.

Rupert also penned the comedy-thriller play *Accomplice*, plus the scripts for *Solitary Confinement*, *Thumbs*, *Marty*, *The First Wives Club*, and *Robin and the 7 Hoods*.

But his hit Broadway musical *The Mystery of Edwin Drood* endeared him most to me. It premiered first in New York City's Central Park at the New York Shakespeare Festival (a product of New York's Public Theater) in 1985. Due to its success at the festival, *Drood* was then transferred to Broadway, where it won five 1986 Tony Awards (including Best Musical, Best Book of a Musical, and Best Original Score). *Drood* ran on Broadway for an amazing year and a half (608 performances), and I was fortunate to see that production.

I was extremely impressed with Rupert's work for *Drood*, not only on the show itself, but because in addition to writing the book, music, and lyrics for it, he wrote the orchestrations. Until *Drood*, only one composer had written book, music, and lyrics for a Broadway musical (Meredith Willson for *The Music Man*), but Rupert was (and is still) the only person to have written book, music, lyrics, *and* orchestrations for a musical. Simply amazing.

Holmes was first encouraged to write a musical by Joseph Papp (founder of New York's Public Theater and its Shakespeare Festival) and Papp's wife after they attended one of Holmes's cabarets in 1983.

The Mystery of Edwin Drood was loosely based on the Charles Dickens unfinished novel of the same name and was inspired by Holmes's memories of English pantomime shows he attended as a child (having been born and reared in England until age six). The Dickens novel is a bit dark and dry by most estimations, so Rupert came up with the ingenious device of setting the story in an English music hall and creating a "show-within-a-show" complete with hilarious, scenery-chewing characters who created a celebrative and highly entertaining evening as they told the story of Edwin Drood.

Because the original novel was left unfinished after Dickens's death, Rupert employed the unusual device of providing alternate endings for each character who is suspected of the murder and letting the audience vote on a different murderer each night. The original production was billed as "The Solve-It-Yourself Broadway Musical." Fantastic!

At last, the evening came when Rupert was to appear at the Nashville bookstore. I grabbed my *Mystery of Edwin Drood* poster and took it with me. I hoped while he was signing his new book for me, he would sign the poster.

At the bookstore, I met up with my dear friends Stan and Janis Gunselman, whom I had invited to join me; they were also Rupert fans. It was standing room only, and Rupert soon appeared to a generous ovation. He sat at a keyboard and launched into several of his hits.

After he'd finished performing and reading excerpts from his new book, he sat behind a table to start signing. I got in line with Stan and Janis. When I reached Rupert, after he signed his new book for me, I put the *Drood* poster in front of him and asked if he might autograph it as well. He smiled and happily obliged. As he signed it, I couldn't resist chatting him up a bit.

"Rupert, I saw *The Mystery of Edwin Drood* on Broadway and loved it. But one of the things that impressed me most about it was that not only did you write book, music, and lyrics for the show, but you also wrote the orchestrations."

"And I'll never do *that* again!" he said, laughing. I was impressed with his humility about his feat that had never been accomplished before nor likely again by anyone else. He could have launched into several ethereal comments about his unique accomplishment, but instead he was down-to-earth and humble about it.

I was so enjoying speaking with him but didn't want to hold up the line, so after he signed my poster, I stepped out of the way for the next person to get his book signed.

It was then when my friend, Stan, opened a door for me. He spoke up: "Rupert, Mark is a music publisher in the print music business."

"Interesting. I have several songs in print," Rupert replied.

Of course, now it was time for me to jump right in. The water seemed to be fine.

"Yes, and I think the songbook for *The Mystery of Edwin Drood* should be back in print and available once again. I would love to help make that happen," I said.

"That would be great, Mark." He nodded to the person standing beside him. "This is Teressa, my assistant. She'll give you her card, and let's talk about it."

Of course, always one to follow up, I called Teressa the following week and discussed the idea of how we might get Rupert's *Drood* songbook back into print. This led to my first lunch with Rupert and Teressa in Manhattan as we worked on getting the songbook ready for its re-release. I'm happy to report the songbook was released and has gone on to sell thousands of copies to *Drood* fans, and it is still selling to this day.

All of this then led to lunch with Rupert in a Scarsdale, New York, restaurant (coincidentally on my birthday – a nice gift that day). We discussed ideas for possible future projects and shared our mutual thoughts about pop music, Broadway, and more.

With such an amazing and far-reaching career, I asked him my burning question: "Rupert, how have you found the time through the years to accomplish *so much*?"

"Well, I had to make a sacrifice in my life and decide I won't get the same amount of sleep that most people get," he said. "People often say to me, 'It's great that you only need three or four hours of sleep per day. That's amazing.' And I tell them, 'No, I actually need eight hours of sleep like everyone else, but there's no way to do what I'm trying to do and get normal hours of sleep.

"There have been times when I've had to work literally seventy-two hours without sleep. I've had to invent extra days in the week. If someone wants to do me a big favor, they'll invent 'Throsday,' which would come in between Tuesday and Wednesday, and that could be my day off," he said with a laugh.

After my lunch with Rupert, I continued to watch his blinding pace of creativity. He wrote the Tony Award–nominated one-man play *Say*

Goodnight, Gracie, based on the relationship between George Burns and Gracie Allen. I saw the show on Broadway…it starred Frank Gorshin (from the 1960s *Batman* TV series). It was an incredible show and performance. Holmes also joined the creative team of the musical *Curtains*, after the deaths of both Peter Stone (the original book writer) and Fred Ebb (the lyricist). Holmes rewrote Stone's original book and contributed additional lyrics to the Kander and Ebb score.

I caught up with Rupert again in 2012 when he was in Nashville for the world premiere production of a new musical version of the classic Jerry Lewis film *The Nutty Professor*. Rupert wrote the book and lyrics for the show while the legendary Marvin Hamlisch wrote the music. Rupert not only took time out of his very busy schedule to visit with me but allowed me to interview him for *Hollywood 360*, the nationally syndicated radio show on which I serve as a correspondent (you can hear the complete interview at www.markcabaniss.com).

I asked him what it was like to work with the legendary Jerry Lewis, who directed this new stage version of the film.

"To work with Jerry Lewis is one of the most astounding experiences I've ever had. One of the most fascinating things is that even now, as he's an octogenarian, every now and then the years will drop away from him, especially if he's demonstrating a comedy bit. And you look, and suddenly you're looking at the Jerry Lewis you grew up with. Or you'll see him make a face, and it's the same face I remember from every Martin and Lewis movie I ever saw.

"It's somewhat like when I was working with Streisand. We would be at the piano chatting, and then I would give her a song I'd just written for her. She would start to sing it, and I'm thinking, *My God, that's Barbra Streisand singing my new song! I know that voice.* So it's the same thing with Jerry. He says things that suddenly remind me of the Jerry Lewis I knew when I was five and thought, *Wouldn't it be great to hang out with that guy?* A truly surreal and out-of-body experience."

When *The Mystery of Edwin Drood* was revived on Broadway for the first time later that year, his assistant Teressa arranged a ticket for me to see the show while I was on a trip to New York City. The show was every bit as entertaining as I remembered it from when I saw it more than twenty-five years earlier. On a subsequent trip to New York a few months later, I saw the show again, and whom should I bump into in the lobby at intermission but Rupert Holmes himself. He immediately stopped and gave me a hug, and we had a nice chat about this latest successful production of one of his creations.

As I settled back into my seat for *Drood*'s second act that evening after chatting with Rupert and the curtain went up, I realized a lot of water had passed under the bridge since I had seen the first production of *Drood* more than twenty-five years earlier. Now I watched the revival of this show with a totally different perspective and with all the more appreciation and respect for its creator. Not only is Rupert Holmes a true *Renaissance man* with an unbelievable combination of unique talent, intelligence, and energy, but he is a genuinely warm and generous human being.

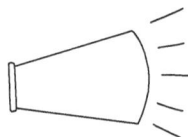

WAIT, WAIT... THERE'S MORE!

To learn more about Rupert Holmes, his writing and music, visit the "semi-official website" at www.rupertholmes.com.

NEW LIGHT SHINING

CAN-DE-LA (NOUN). A UNIT OF LUMINOUS INTENSITY, DEFINED AS THE LUMINOUS INTENSITY OF A SOURCE THAT EMITS MONOCHROMATIC RADIATION OF FREQUENCY 540 X 10 HERTZ.

I've always liked the word *light*. I like what it represents and the visual images it evokes for me. To me, light is bright, hope, no fear, truth, freedom, authenticity, and a number of other positive thoughts and emotions. And although I occasionally enjoy a rainy day, I love the bright, sunny ones most.

So when I came across the word *candela* many years ago, the sound of it struck me. It obviously sounds like *candle*, so I investigated and found that *candela* is the Latin origin of the English word *candle*. No surprise. The luminous intensity of a typical candle is approximately one *candela*.

Since the onset of my adventures in the music business beginning with *Break Forth Into Joy*, I had often dreamed of starting my own company. Even before the winds of change began to blow at Word, I knew it was time for me to seriously pursue that dream (hence my pursuit of buying Shawnee Press and Alfred's church music division). I knew I wasn't getting any younger (funny how that works), and my biological career clock was ticking. CandelaWorks was a name I'd toyed with for a few years as a possible name of my eventual company, so I contacted my attorney and formed a new LLC: CandelaWorks Music.

Next, I approached Word about purchasing Jubilate Music, the print music division I had founded at Word. Jubilate (pronounced *YOO-buh-lah-tay*) had experienced double-digit growth each year since I started it in 2010, so it was a plum catalog for anyone to own. It was my "baby," and it would be nice to hang on to it. I had left other "babies" of mine behind at other publishers in the past due to various circumstances, so I was determined to keep this one if at all possible.

Once again, I brought in my attorney and business advisor to discuss the acquisition of a music publisher. After failed attempts at buying Shawnee Press and Alfred church music, I feared they would think this was yet another overpriced proposition and pass on helping me out. Fortunately, they signed on again with their usual enthusiasm, and we were back at the due diligence stage. After about a month of negotiations, Word and I arrived on a mutually agreeable purchase price for Jubilate Music. So, as far as my purchasing a music publisher, the third time was indeed the charm! The day I signed the contract to buy it will always be the second happiest day of my career. The happiest day comes later in this chapter.

As these new options were being put into place, my old friend the phone rang one afternoon. On the other end were the president/CEO, CFO, and CMO (chief marketing officer) of Alfred Music, calling from Los Angeles. The music business is ultimately a small community, and my friends at Alfred had also heard change was in the wind. We discussed our recent round of negotiations to buy the Alfred church music division, and then they asked if I might be interested in a different scenario wherein I would create a joint venture with Alfred Music (which could include Jubilate Music) and join the Alfred team to head up their church music division.

The music business is about ups and downs and sideways and backwards and all-the-way-around-wards. You can be an award winner one day and nowhere the next. It can be a champagne reception one month and a hard candy Christmas the next. It can all change in an instant and often does.

And so change it did, once again. I signed on with Alfred and brought Jubilate with me. I immediately got busy with the next chapter, never having a chance to look back or catch my breath. I was thrilled to transition back to the educational/church side of the music publishing world and happy to be connected to the team at Alfred, with Morty and Iris Manus, my dear friends whom I and many others appreciate and respect so very much.

Fast forward to late 2015, over two years after signing on at Alfred. Morty Manus passed away, and change was once again in the wind. Alfred had struggled with cash flow for years since its acquisition of Warner Bros. Publications (although had held on valiantly and successfully, by the skin of its teeth). So when a large company in Colorado (Peaksware, owner of the wildly successful music engraving software Finale) approached Ron Manus (son of Morty and Iris) about purchasing Alfred Music, the deal was eventually done. But Ron, loyal friend that he was (and is) remembered my question to him and his parents before signing on with Alfred a few years prior: "Would you ever consider selling your church music division to me?" I had asked. And so, during negotiations with Peaksware, Ron carved out the Alfred Sacred division (and its associated sacred catalogs, including Jubilate Music) and sold it to me (with Peaksware's blessing). The deal became effective on January 1, 2016, and my next exciting adventure in the music business took off. The happiest day of my career!

I named my company Jubilate Music Group, and the "group" contained Alfred Sacred, Jubilate Music, and the venerable H.W. Gray publishing catalog (founded in 1906). There have been additional exciting acquisitions I've done since then to add to the company. I've found owning copyrights is a bit like Lay's potato chips: You can't eat just one.

Having my own company has been the hardest work I've done in my entire career. Period. But I can say without reservation, it is the most fun I've ever had in my career. I can't imagine there will be another major chapter for me in my career at my stage in life. And I'm not only fine with that, I'm also deeply grateful that this "grand finale" for me as regards music publishing is the most satisfying by far.

I named one of my catalogs at Jubilate "CandelaWorks Music." I defined "Candela" at the beginning of this chapter as regards light. And the publications we release at Jubilate Music Group are truly filled with light and are reaching people literally around the world. One definition of Jubilate is "a song of joy and triumph." That it has truly been for me, I'm deeply grateful to write.

I am reminded of a quotation that has often inspired me in my various quests, from the man who invented the light bulb:

>"Vision without execution is hallucination."
>—*Thomas Edison*

GUYS AND DOLLS AND FEUER AND MARTIN

As far as places to visit are concerned, New York City is my favorite city in the world. I'm always happy when I'm there, even if it's in the dead of winter. So although it was a dead winter afternoon in NYC, I was particularly excited to be there because I was scheduled to meet Cy Feuer, who was called "The Last Great Broadway Showman." I jumped out of the cab in the Lincoln Center area of Manhattan and rushed into a nice apartment building. I greeted the doorman inside the warm lobby and told him I was there to see Cy Feuer. My mind was simultaneously running on another track. I had suddenly become age fifteen all over again.

The very first musical in which I ever participated as a performer (at age fifteen) was the classic *Guys and Dolls*. It was our high school musical my sophomore year, long before the TV movie *High School Musical*—along with Zac Efron and Disney—made high school musicals cool. With music and lyrics by Frank Loesser and book by Jo Swerling and Abe Burrows (more on Jo Swerling later), it was based on a story by Damon Runyon, a late, great newspaperman and short story writer.

Even as a naïve fifteen-year-old sophomore, I noticed that the script, cast album, and posters for *Guys and Dolls* had "Feuer and Martin present..." above the title of the show. *Just who are Feuer and Martin?* I was interested to know. I would find out decades later. Had there not been a Cy Feuer, there would not have been a *Guys and Dolls*.

Cy Feuer was an American theatre producer, director, composer, musician, and half of the legendary producing duo Feuer and Martin. He was the winner of three Tony Awards plus a lifetime achievement Tony.

Born Seymour Arnold Feuerman in Brooklyn, he became a professional trumpet player at the age of fifteen, working at clubs on weekends to help support his family while attending high school. It was there he first met Abe Burrows, who in later years he would hire to write the book for *Guys and Dolls*. Having no interest in mathematics, science, or sports, he dropped out of school and found work as a trumpet player on a political campaign truck. He later studied at the Juilliard School before joining the orchestras at the Roxy Theater and later Radio City Music Hall. In 1938, he toured the country with Leon Belasco and his orchestra, eventually ending up in Burbank, California. Following a ten-week stint there, the orchestra departed for Minneapolis, but Feuer opted to remain in California.

There, Feuer found employment at Republic Pictures, serving as musical director, arranger, and/or composer of more than 125 mostly B-movies, many of them serials and westerns, for the next decade, except for a three-year interruption to serve in the military during World War II. During his Hollywood sojourn, he enjoyed a tumultuous one-year affair with actress Susan Hayward, worked with Jule Styne, Frank Loesser, and Victor Young, among others, and received five Academy Award nominations for his film scores.

In 1947, having decided he had no real talent for film scoring (even though he'd received five Oscar nominations!), Feuer returned to New York City, where he teamed up with Ernest H. Martin, who had been the head of comedy programming at CBS Radio. After an aborted attempt to stage a production based on George Gershwin's *An American in Paris*, they produced *Where's Charley?*, the 1949 Frank Loesser adaptation of *Charley's Aunt*. Although six of the seven major New York critics panned it, positive word of mouth about the show, particularly Ray Bolger's star turn in it, kept it running for three years. Over the next several decades, Feuer and Martin mounted some of the most notable titles in the Broadway musical canon, including *Guys and Dolls* and *How to Succeed in Business Without Really Trying*, both of which won the Tony Award for Best Musical. As of this writing, *How to Succeed...* is one of only seven musicals to have won the Pulitzer Prize for Drama.

Feuer was also a stage director. Among his Broadway directing credits were *Little Me* and the ill-fated *I Remember Mama*. Feuer's greatest career success was the 1972 film version of *Cabaret*, which won eight Academy Awards, winning him a Best Picture Oscar nomination as the film's credited producer. (*Cabaret* lost Best Picture to *The Godfather*, but Feuer won a Golden Globe for Best Motion Picture, Musical or Comedy.) With Martin, he was responsible for the 1985 screen adaptation of *A Chorus Line*, which proved to be one of their biggest flops. In addition to his producing, Feuer served as president, and later chairman, of the League of American Theatres and Producers (now called The Broadway League) from 1989 to 2003.

So to say he'd had a busy career would be an understatement.

The elevator door opened onto the twenty-fourth floor, and I stepped off to find the apartment. I rang the bell and was greeted by a housekeeper, who led me in to meet...*ta da*...Cy Feuer. He smiled and warmly welcomed me.

Mr. Feuer was dressed in a smart blue blazer and slacks, crisp shirt, and ascot. He led me to their beautiful living room, replete with Broadway memorabilia, awards, and the like. We sat, and his wife, Posy, joined us and also greeted me cordially.

Here was a man of elegance and style, even at the age of ninety-one. His wit and mind were seemingly as sharp as ever. I was there simply because here was a part of Broadway history I wanted to meet and, through my connections with that world, had landed this meeting. I had also thought that the meeting might develop into an article that I would write for a magazine or website (or book!), so I was ready to take careful notes.

"Make yourself comfortable, Mark," he said as he offered me something to drink. His Brooklyn accent was not erased after years of being a world traveler.

"It's an honor to meet you and Mrs. Feuer," I said.

"Please call me Cy," he replied.

Well now, I thought, *this boy from North Carolina is officially on a first-name basis with the Last Great Broadway Showman.*

After settling in, I got right to it. Of course, being a fan of Meredith Willson and *The Music Man*, I knew that Cy Feuer and Ernie Martin had almost been the producers of that show.

"I would love to talk about a lot of things this afternoon," I started, "but I can't resist starting with the story that…according to Meredith Willson in his book *But He Doesn't Know the Territory*…the book about how he wrote *The Music Man*…he credits you with coming up with the name of his show."

"That's right. Meredith wanted to call the show 'The Silver Triangle,' but Ernie and I weren't crazy about that title. We told Mere that he needed a million-dollar name for his show, and 'The Silver Triangle' was not it.

"So after Mere had written yet another draft of the show, Ernie and I went out to Los Angeles to see Mere and Rini, as we were thinking we were going to produce the show, and when we drove up in their driveway, as they came out of the door to greet us, I didn't say hello or anything… I just shouted out, 'The Music Man. That's your title, Mere.' And Mere immediately said, 'I like it fine.' Then he looked at Rini, who said, 'Me too.' And that was that."

He continued about *The Music Man*:

"Of course, Ernie and I regret that it didn't work out for us to produce *The Music Man*, but the timing wasn't right. Mere, Rini, Ernie, and I all remained close friends, and Ernie and I were delighted by the success of the show."

I had to get to *Guys and Dolls* next. "How did that show come about?"

"One day I got a call from Ernie, who was in California on some family errand, and he told me that his wife, Nancy, was in bed reading an anthology of Damon Runyon stories called *Guys and Dolls*. 'That's it,' I said. I didn't have to hear any more. I had already heard the title of our next show.

"We then contacted Frank [Loesser] to see if he would consider writing the score. Frank said, 'I'm in. I love Runyon.' And Frank went straight ahead to write a song, even without knowing the plot yet. He was also inspired by the title of the show. He wrote a terrific piece of music as a round for three guys. Frank called it 'Fugue for Tinhorns,' but Ernie and I eventually just called it 'Can Do.'"

Of course, Frank Loesser's "Fugue for Tinhorns" has become a standard in the musical theatre canon.

"Next, we had to find a story to attach to Frank's song. It arrived sometime in the spring of 1949: 'The Idyll of Miss Sarah Brown,' a Runyon gem."

In "The Idyll of Miss Sarah Brown," Sergeant Sarah Brown was running the Save-a-Soul Mission, loosely based on the Salvation Army, which was particularly unsuccessful in attracting sinners in spite of the fact that it was situated in the heart of sinful Manhattan. The Mission was so bad at doing good that the regional general was coming to town to decide whether to keep the Mission open. When the biggest gambler in town, Sky Masterson, heard of this great moral crisis at a local crap game, he offered the following bet to all the gamblers: "I will put up cash and you will put up a marker. If I lose, you win cash. If I win, you will have to attend one prayer meeting." Sky won the bet, and the colorful gamblers had to attend the prayer meeting, thus saving the Mission. Sarah fell under Sky's spell, which led to the unlikely love story: a gambler and a missionary. As a strong subplot, they blended the story of gambler Nathan Detroit and his long-time fiancée, dancer Miss Adelaide.

But next, Feuer and Martin needed a book writer to weave all these elements together with the necessary stage directions and dialog. So they called Jo Swerling to write the script (or libretto, as it's called).

"Swerling had a big house in Malibu and a huge string of film credits… *It's a Wonderful Life, A Lady Takes a Chance, The Pride of the Yankees*…a big talent," said Cy as he sipped on a Perrier with a twist of lime.

Swerling wrote the first draft of *Guys and Dolls* and was very pleased with it.

"But we were still missing some suspense and tension in the show," he said. "Ernie finally cracked the problem. He said the bet needed to be more than just getting the boys to a prayer meeting. The stakes had to be higher."

Cy continued, "It hit me. It was an old plot, but it might work here too. So I said, 'What if there's one dance hall beauty who never gives any of the sailors in the fleet a tumble? Finally, one of the sailors – a real ladies' man – bets that he can break the ice. Everyone in the fleet gets in on the bet.' But Jo didn't think it was necessary or quite got it.

"'That's the bet!' I said to Swerling. 'Sky Masterson makes a bet that he can take a tumble with Sarah Brown. That's how he gets all the gamblers to come to the Mission!'"

Feuer and Martin loved it. Swerling was highly indignant and protested, "You want me to steal a plot, somebody else's work! I will not do it. I have my reputation, my honor."

Cy said Swerling went on and on about his honor while they tried to convince him that this plot had been used – in various forms and places – again and again. Swerling wouldn't even agree to find his own variation on the plot or acknowledge that a high stakes bet was essential to the characters of the people who would inhabit the world of *Guys and Dolls*. So Feuer and Martin parted ways with Jo Swerling.

"We realized he was the wrong guy for us. We finally had to fire him, although he insisted that he still receive top billing in the credits for the play and retain some small percentage of the royalties. This in spite of the fact that *not one* of his words ever appeared in the show."

Feuer and Martin then approached Abe Burrows to write the libretto for the show.

"He had everything I wanted. Not only was he a high school classmate, he had a very down-to-earth yet erudite wit."

It took some convincing from Cy to lure Burrows away from a well-paying, steady job as head writer on a very popular NBC radio show at the time, *Duffy's Tavern*. But Feuer and Martin eventually got their man. The ultimate result was irresistible. And a smash Broadway hit.

Guys and Dolls opened on Broadway on November 24, 1950, and ran for

1,200 performances. As I sat with this Broadway legend, I thought I should ask something that possibly only he could remember about the opening night of this classic show. He didn't hesitate as he shared another anecdote and he freshened my glass of Perrier. While he told the story, it was as if he was there all over again, enjoying the excitement of such an auspicious opening night.

"I'll never forget the first few moments of the overture," he said. "I took Posy's hand when the music started." Cy and Posy smiled at each other as he spoke. "In the show's overture, there's that trumpet solo that is the classic 'call to the post' you hear at horse races. Well, when the audience heard that, they started laughing. At that moment, I looked at Posy and said, 'We've got 'em!'"

The Great Broadway Showman knew that if he could grab the audience's attention and interest as early as the overture, they had a chance of holding that audience throughout the show. And hold that audience they did on that night in November 1950, right through the final curtain.

Guys and Dolls has since continued to hold audiences year in and year out – for more than sixty years. Feuer and Martin truly "got us."

Cy Feuer died on May 17, 2006, at the age of ninety-five. But *Guys and Dolls* and the other theatre classics he and Ernest Martin produced continue to entertain millions through film and stage each year.

As for Broadway Showmen, indeed, they don't make 'em like that anymore.

I CAN SEE KATHIE LEE

There aren't many celebrities whom you know they are by simply saying their first name.

Prince. Elvis. Cher. Beyonce. Bono.

Then there's Kathie Lee. (Well, I guess that's two names, but you could say she's a "two-name one namer"). Kathie Lee is instantly known by her first name only. And that's quite an honor for any celebrity. And who doesn't seem to know the name Kathie Lee?

To start with, Kathie Lee Gifford has logged in literally thousands of hours on television. It began for her as TV gameshow host Tom Kennedy's singer/sidekick on the syndicated version of *Name That Tune* (1977–1978). Later in 1978, she joined the cast of the short-lived *Hee Haw* spinoff, *Hee Haw Honeys*. She was also a correspondent and substitute anchor on ABC-TV's *Good Morning America* in the early 1980s. Kathie's career took off even more so in the 80s as a vocalist on the ABC game show *Face the Music* with Ron Ely. Also in the 80s she appeared on the first three hours of *Today* as a contributing NBC News correspondent.

But then, her biggest career break happened when on June 24, 1985 she replaced Ann Abernathy as co-host of *The Morning Show* on New York City's WABC-TV with Regis Philbin. The program eventually went into national broadcast in 1988 as *Live! With Regis and Kathie Lee* and Kathie became well known across the country. Throughout the 1990s, morning-TV viewers enjoyed her descriptions of life at home with her sportscaster husband Frank Gifford, son Cody, and daughter Cassidy. They had no script on that show, especially during the extended opening segment. It was Kathie and Regis unfettered, talking about life and everything else. And the public ate it up. Their back and forth banter and merciless kidding and joking together was unrehearsed and totally real. And the public knew it was authentic. Never had a morning show of that type exhibited such spontaneity, wit, and ease. The chemistry between Kathie Lee and Regis was hilarious, unpredictable, and genuine. Regis and Kathie Lee set a new standard for morning television.

Accordingly, the co-hosts were jointly nominated eight years in a row (1993 to 2000) for Outstanding Talk Show Host during the Daytime Emmy Awards. But even while at the top of her game, Kathie did the unpredictable once again: She decided to leave the show in 2000. She explained that filling in for Carol Burnett on Broadway and guest-hosting *The Late Show with David Letterman* had inspired her to pursue more challenging work. The day after she hosted *Late Show* on February 24, 2000, she told Regis she had decided to leave *Live!* Her last episode aired on July 28, 2000.

For the next eight years, Kathie took on new and challenging projects as a performer, producer, writer, and more. Then, her television destiny came calling again.

On March 31, 2008, NBC announced that Kathie was to join its morning show, *Today,* as co-host of the fourth hour to be titled *Today with Kathie Lee and Hoda.* Alongside NBC's Hoda Kotb, this marked Kathie's return to morning television. In the weeks prior to her arrival, ratings indicated 1.9 million viewers of the fourth hour of *Today.* But when Kathie joined the show, ratings doubled. Once again, she had created "must-see TV" for her millions of fans.

And now this television icon was walking down a tarmac at the Nashville airport to meet me.

I CAN SEE KATHIE LEE

I was at a secluded portion of the airport where private jets arrive. Kathie had arrived on such a jet with her assistant (Christine) to meet with me on that day and I can still remember standing at the door of that special greeting area as she stepped off the plane with Christine and started walking towards me. It's one thing to look at someone through your television set for some 30 plus years but then to see her heading your way live and in person is quite another. "I can see Kathie Lee!" was the thought that ran through my mind. And for the first time ever, she could see me, too.

And what I have learned in the years I have known Kathie Lee since that first meeting is what you see is what you get. She is refreshingly as consistent off the air as she is on. No pretense or different personality. She is truly the real deal. So while I could see "the real" Kathie Lee for the first time that day, you do too whenever you see her on television.

My meeting Kathie had its beginnings about a year prior, when I was having lunch with my banker friend Lisa Harless. Lisa is a Music City Legend as the (now retired) head of the music and entertainment division of a major bank in Nashville. We had met years before and hit it off immediately (everyone hits it off with Lisa). One time during one of my many lunches with her, she mentioned in passing something about her friend David Pomeranz, and then proceeded to finish her story. I said "Wait a minute. Rewind. You just said you know David Pomeranz? I would love to meet him! I'm a huge fan of his songwriting for decades." *Footnote: I could write a chapter on the enormously multi-talented, award-winning David Pomeranz, but I suggest you go to www.davidpomeranz.com to learn more about him. He's simply amazing. And a super nice guy on top of it all. You'll be astounded by his hit songs that you know recorded by a who's who of top artists: Barry Manilow, Freddie Mercury, Bette Midler, Kenny Loggins, Glen Campbell, Donna Summer, Cliff Richard, and many others.*

Soon after my lunch with Lisa, thanks to her making it happen, there I was sitting across the table having lunch with none other than David Pomeranz, talking with him as if we'd known each other for years. And I felt as if I did know him since I know his music so well. Not long after that first meeting with him, he said on a subsequent meeting as we brainstormed on various project ideas, "I want to introduce you to my friend Kathie Lee Gifford." Kathie was getting more involved in writing songs at this point in her career, and me being a music publisher, David thought we would be a good match. So he went about setting up a phone call for Kathie and me.

So not long after that first fun call with Kathie, there she was coming down the tarmac and I was soon making the rounds with her at several Nashville music publishing offices I had set up for her. They loved her, and her songs. Little did I know, but she was quite taken with Nashville once again. She had lived in Nashville for stretches during her *Hee Haw Honeys* days. And now, it appeared the Nashville bug was biting her again (but it wouldn't be for several years before she added a Nashville home to her places of residence) . While I was at one publisher's office, which was also in the record business, I said to them (knowing they produced children's recordings and Kathie Lee had written some children's books): "Would you be interested in turning one of Kathie's children's books into a recording?" Without hesitation, they answered enthusiastically "Yes!"

Therefore, at lunch right after our meetings that morning, I told Kathie that while she was chatting with others at one of the publishers we visited that morning, I had pitched the idea of turning one of her children's books into a recording with new songs written by her. She liked the idea and said she wanted to think more about it for a few days after she had returned home. Indeed, a few days after she returned home, I got a call from her. "Mark, I've thought about the children's idea but instead of doing a recording on one of my books, I would rather do a project called 'The Little Giant.'"

On one of her trips to the Holy Land, Kathie and her husband Frank Gifford had been challenged by their tour guide in the Valley of Elah – where David slew Goliath – to throw a stone from the ground. Then the tour guide asked, "What is *your* stone? What is your gift or power that you will use to change the world for good?" This inspired Kathie to write the lyrics to "What Is Your Stone?" for which David Pomeranz set to music.

On her call to me, Kathie then proceeded to spin out the ideas her fertile mind had created since I'd last seen her in Nashville. The children's record would use "What Is Your Stone?" as its core, and would be the story of David and Goliath, but with a twist.

"The story is told by a sheep named Sheba…you know, David was a shepherd…so his lead sheep tells the story from her perspective."

I was loving this. There are really no females in the story of David and Goliath, and she had invented an organic way to bring some in.

"But Sheba's a few of Sheba's sheep friends have a little problem with flatulence."

"Oh, really?" I responded.

"You know how little kids go bananas whenever that happens, and they think it's the funniest thing ever" she replied. I couldn't disagree with that.

"I'll get Regis (Philbin) to play the part of Jesse and some Broadway performer friends to play other parts," she added.

I was dizzy at this point thinking about the possibilities that were stacking up. Regis Philbin, no less!

Well, to fast forward to about a month later, I found myself on the set of the *Today* Show waiting for Kathie to "get off work" so we could go to her home in Connecticut and work on *The Little Giant*. I watched her do her magic on the show as I stood behind the cameras. That was quite an experience in and of itself, and the first of several times I met her at the show often sitting in the Green Room first where celebrities congregate before they appear on the show, then going on set and watching the show from behind the cameras, then waiting outside her dressing room until she changed into her street clothes, then exiting an obscure side door from NBC Studios where no one would really notice her, where the NBC Limousine was waiting for us about 10 steps from the door. The limo then drove us straight to her home in Greenwich, Connecticut (about a 45-minute drive from Midtown Manhattan). Talk about fun and heady days!

Kathie's home (one of several she owns in different cities in the US) is simply breathtaking. It sits on a little peninsula of sorts and if you squint when standing in her large backyard, you can see the skyscrapers on lower

Manhattan. Beautiful yachts and sailboats dotted the water surrounding the peninsula. I could write a chapter on that home. It was large, to say the least, and decorated with every beautiful touch you can imagine. But it had such a warm and inviting feel in every room. You could tell here was a home where the Giffords had lived for years…a family…with all their joys and celebrations, challenges, and triumphs. A generous number of framed photographs populate the home basically documenting their family life. Beautiful, fun pictures. And by the time I arrived on the scene, it was where Frank Gifford had passed away a few months before. I wish I had gotten to meet Frank, but it was not meant to be. So there was sadness in my mind regarding that aspect of things. But Kathie was upbeat always. She said "People say to me, 'Oh I'm so sorry you lost Frank' but I say 'I didn't lose him…I know exactly where he is and he's happy.' "

We had some free time before dinner after one of our writing sessions, and she said I could rest in my room, or make phone calls or walk around – whatever I wanted. She said she was going to her exercise room to work out. I asked her if I could join her and she said "Absolutely!" but then I confessed "But I don't have any workout clothing." She said, "No problem, you can wear some of Frank's stuff." And I thought "Now how cool is that!? She's offering me to work out in legendary pro football and broadcaster Frank Gifford's own gear!" So it took me all of 2 seconds to say "Yes!"

The "exercise room" was actually a small independent little brick place that was like a small health club unto itself. Next to their outdoor tennis courts. We worked out and had a blast talking about fitness. I was impressed with how she worked out. She wasn't just playing around, she made it a worthwhile session. No wonder she looked so good on TV!

Afterwards, when I said I would promptly change out of the Frank Gifford gear so she could launder it she said "Oh you can keep it. He doesn't need it anymore."

I'll never forget during one of my stays there, her daughter Cassidy was spending the weekend and one morning we ended up at the breakfast table together while Kathie was at NBC doing her show. Cassidy was so wonderful, genuine, and truly sweet and kind. Another time, her son, Cody called, and Kathie had him on speaker phone when I walked into the room. She never announced that I was there overhearing their conversation, and he was so kind, respectful, and loving to his mother. Even though he was unaware I was there. My subsequent connections with Cody have always been delightful. He and Cassidy are truly beautiful people. Frank and Kathie Lee did a wonderful job as parents.

There are more wonderful stories of dinners there, and other visits to finish up *The Little Giant*, let alone the actual recording sessions themselves, but suffice it to say it was a fabulous, wonderful, and unforgettable time. I'm so very proud of the project *The Little Giant* and how it turned out. Such fun, and whenever l occasionally take it out to listen to it, I can't help but smile and get a deep sense of joy knowing how it all happened.

There have been many more encounters with Kathie Lee since those early ones, especially since she moved to Nashville. And we've talked about other projects which will hopefully develop in the future. I would love to work with her again at that level. She's a consummate professional and very talented. And an absolute hoot.

She gave her Connecticut home to Cody and his wife where they are raising their children now. What an incredibly generous thing to do. But that's Kathie. Because I can see Kathie Lee. And you can, too.

SOLI DEO GLORIA

Growing up in Shelby, I can still remember listening to the various records (*yes, records!*) of the musicals in which I was involved at my home church at different times. I always faithfully read the producing credits on the album jacket. I learned a lot, actually, through reading those credits, and my dreams of working in the music publishing business began right there in my living room in front of the stereo (that looked like a piece of furniture back then). I usually never forget a name, and I didn't forget the many names of composers, arrangers, producers, narrators, and singers… even recording engineers…on those projects. I hoped to work with those talented people someday.

When I was seventeen, I worked up enough courage to pick up the phone and call a hero (I'm telling you, I have never been afraid to use that phone, even as a seventeen-year-old). The hero was Mark Blankenship, and I was quite taken with his composing, arrangements, and orchestrations on several church musicals I'd sung in my church youth choir. So I decided I was going to call him and find out more about how he did what he did.

I called what seemed like a foreign and magical music place, Nashville, where I figured out Mark Blankenship worked. I got through to him, and he was encouraging and kind to an interested kid. Years later, once I had gotten into the music business, I became good friends with Mark. He published some of my music, I published some of his, and he, his wife, Judy, and I got to know each other well though various music conventions. I keep in touch with Mark, and we remain good friends to this day.

And then when I was in college at Mars Hill, my junior year our college choir went on a cross-country trip to New Mexico. That was the first time I ever laid eyes on Nashville. As we drove west on Interstate 40 that sunny day, when I saw the Nashville skyline, I said quietly to myself, "I want to live here someday and work in the music business."

While I was in college, I also got to know and love the music of David Danner. Here was another consummate musician…songwriter, arranger, and orchestrator. During my graduate school years at the University of Tennessee, I decided I would write my master's thesis on a music publisher and drove to Nashville from Knoxville early one cold February morning to research possibly writing my thesis on Nashville-based Broadman Press. With one call to Mark Blankenship, he arranged for me to observe two days of a recording session on a choral project that had been orchestrated by David Danner. David would be in the studio to conduct, and another name I'd seen on countless recordings as producer, Sharron Lyon, would produce.

Mark gave me directions over the phone on how to get to the studio, and I could hardly contain my excitement. I drove from Knoxville to Nashville early that morning. I got to the studio as the professional musicians were also arriving, and soon, the red light blinked on, the tape rolled, and David Danner gave the downbeat to the orchestra.

It was incredible! The sounds coming over the large speakers in the control room where I was sitting that sounded so professional weren't coming from that home stereo in Shelby. They were coming "live" from the room on the other side of the large glass window! The process of multi-track recording immediately fascinated me.

Sharron Lyon (the name I knew so well from reading those recording credits) was smooth and professional. Observing her, I started to understand the role of a producer and how she helped shape the recording. She was very encouraging to me in my career that day, as was David Danner. Sharron, David, and his wife, Judy, and I had lunch. It was such a momentous occasion for me, I can still remember vividly where we went and not only what I had to eat but what everyone else had! Mark Blankenship, being a fine singer in addition to his composing and orchestration talents, sang the next day on the vocal session. Once again, Mark was encouraging to me in my career. And because of my faithful reading of those album credits, I recognized several of the singers by name when I met them.

As I drove back to Knoxville from this defining experience, I knew how I wanted to spend my foreseeable future: in the sacred music publishing business.

And I have.

My many adventures in the music business would not have been possible through the years had it not been for my primary means of making a living – that being the sacred music publishing industry. Those contacts have led to many more in seemingly somewhat unrelated fields, such as broadcasting or Broadway. But inspiring mentors such as Meredith Willson, Steven Allen, and Loonis McGlohon proved to me it can be done. And my passion for publishing music for the church has remained strong through the years.

As noted earlier, my first published composition "Break Forth Into Joy" opened a lot of doors for me, and – as Meredith Willson used to say, according to his wife – one thing leads to another. That surely and thankfully has been the case in my career.

Shortly after moving to Nashville to work for Brentwood Music in 1989, I sought out David Danner to work with him. I eventually connected with David, and he vaguely remembered that young grad student who had sat in on his recording session years earlier. I went on to publish several of his pieces, including two musicals. Working with David and getting to know him as a dear friend have been career highlights for me. David passed away in 1992, and as Providence would have it, I saw him on the day he died at his home. Neither of us knew that would be his final day. His last words to me were, "Love you, my friend."

Sharron Lyon, the producer of those countless recordings I heard in high school and beyond (and editor of hundreds of thousands of notes during her distinguished career), has become a dear friend and mentor, whom I see on a regular basis. She still encourages and guides me in my career.

Rewinding to my high school years. I was occasionally asked to narrate our youth choir cantatas. During my senior year I was asked to narrate a children's musical titled *Beauty and the Feast* (the biblical story of Esther). It was written by Grace Hawthorne and Charles F. Brown, and it also became a defining moment for me. The songs of the musical were particularly clever and inspiring (thanks to its writers) and made an indelible impression on me. Being one who noticed everything about print music even back in those days, I was also drawn to the cover of the musical. It had a beautifully painted illustration montage of the major characters from the story of Esther: Haman, Mordecai, and King Ahasuerus, with Esther in the center. It was truly striking.

Years later, I sought out both Grace Hawthorne and Charles F. (Charlie) Brown to write for me. They did so (separately, as it worked out) on various projects, including musicals. I found them to be very talented, filled with great ideas, and absolutely delightful. Charlie has since retired from writing, but Grace has continued, now adding novelist to her impressive resume. Grace and her husband live in Atlanta, and on a recent trip there, Grace – knowing what her *Beauty and the Feast* musical means to me – presented me at dinner with the actual artwork used on the cover of the book as a gift! In its original form, it's actually a large, beautiful painting and naturally, even more striking than the reproduction of it on the book's cover. The painting is framed and hangs in my home, often reminding me of the main message of the musical, "Everything works out right when you trust in God." In 2022, I co-wrote – with Mark Blankenship – a concert musical titled *Triumph of Faith: The Musical Story of Esther* which received its world premiere at Carnegie Hall in July of that year to a standing ovation. You can't make this stuff up.

The other great treasure of my career in sacred music publishing is having known, worked with, and become close friends with the one and only Buryl Red.

I had known the name Buryl Red for as long as I could remember. When I was a teenager in my church's youth choir, like millions of others, we performed Buryl's "pulpit musical drama" *Celebrate Life*. He had co-written it with Ragan Courtney back in 1972, and it had become an enduring classic, as so much of Buryl's work did.

Buryl was yet another one of my "hyphenated" friends. He was a composer-conductor-arranger-producer-orchestrator. So in 1997, I took a deep breath and picked up the phone and called him to write for me. Our first conversation lasted about an hour because we immediately connected. That began one long conversation that lasted until a week before he passed away in 2013, the last time I spoke to him.

Buryl wrote several things for me, which I published, all of which were highly creative and commercially successful. Buryl was aptly described by *The Washington Post* as "uncommonly creative." His musical work was heard in such diverse venues as Carnegie Hall, *Saturday Night Live*, and thousands of schools, churches, and theaters around the world. His output included more than sixteen hundred published compositions and arrangements, production of more than 2,500 recordings, and the musical supervision, composition, and arranging for several hundred shows, documentaries, and musical specials for network and cable television. Of his choral works, *Celebrate Life* and the first performing edition of Pergolesi's *Magnificat* are considered landmarks in their fields. With Grace Hawthorne, he wrote the classic children's musical *It's Cool in the Furnace*, which – after over forty years – remains in print and is still performed around the world to this day.

One of Buryl's greatest passions was arranging music for and conducting *The CenturyMen*, a 100-voice men's choir (consisting of an auditioned group of church music directors from coast to coast). I traveled many times to see them whenever they toured within driving distance of Nashville. Their performances were always stunning and inspirational. Buryl always brought incredible and amazing music out of that group.

Having lived in New York City most of his adult life, Buryl became very connected and respected in Broadway circles. He orchestrated several Broadway musicals and served as a music consultant for many more. He introduced me to many luminaries in that field, arranged for me to walk the red carpet at a Broadway musical opening night, and skillfully guided me through the process of getting my own musicals reviewed and/or produced by top-rate producers. But mostly, Buryl became a trusted close friend and confidant. We never ran out of things to say to each other.

Buryl passed away on April 1, 2013, after a long battle with cancer. Since he knew he was terminally ill, he helped plan his own memorial service. And what a service it was in New York City! It was a who's who of Broadway, music, and the arts, with *The CenturyMen* singing as well. I was deeply honored that Buryl chose me as one of the speakers to eulogize him that night.

I often told Buryl his music is timeless. He simply smiled and thanked me, with typical humility. Like all great composers, Buryl's music reflected him and his timelessness. Buryl Red lives forever not only in eternity, but through his music. Whenever I hear his music now, it's as if I'm having a conversation with him. And I miss him.

My shameless name-dropping list and anecdotes of Christian artists and writers whom I've had—and continue to have—the great joy and honor of working with over the years could continue. People such as Cynthia Clawson, Ragan Courtney, Ken Medema, Kurt Kaiser, John Purifoy, and others.

The word *artist* is tossed around so freely in the music business. But all of the people I've mentioned in this chapter are truly consummate *artists*. They have changed and enriched my life (and millions of others) in profound and eternal ways. The incredible and deeply satisfying experiences with all of them make any bad day I've ever had (or ever will) in my career well worth it.

And for that I say, *Soli Deo Gloria*…Glory to God alone.

EPILOGUE: THE MUSIC OF LIFE

I agree with Meredith Willson that life has rhythm, harmony, and melody to it, and the daily sounds – and people – around us (if we listen closely enough) are like music unto themselves. If we have the faith to believe before seeing, we can indeed see the band and hear the music of life.

So when I was commissioned to write a choral anthem that was to commemorate the 30th anniversary of the building of the Malcolm E. Brown Auditorium at my high school alma mater, I reached into the part of me that believes in the rhythm and music of life and how the transforming power of music ultimately lies within us all. Like others, I had spent countless – and very happy – hours at that auditorium making music in musicals, plays, concerts, rehearsals, and other events during high school, college, and beyond. So this facility held (and will always hold) a very special place in my heart. Accordingly, a piece with music itself as the theme emerged. The result was *And There Is Music*.

The premiere of the anthem on a Sunday afternoon in the auditorium by the school's combined chorus, band, and orchestra was one of those unforgettable occasions for me. I've attended numerous premieres of pieces I've written over the years, but this one was particularly special. The auditorium was filled, and the song received a standing ovation. I suspect the ovation was more for the wonderful performance of the musicians and deservedly so (but perhaps also a little for their native son!). I will always be thankful to the audience and performers that day for making me so happy and grateful in that moment.

And on any crystal-clear fall morning, or whenever I see the world's wonderful horizon, mountains, or beach, I feel as if I'm twenty-three years old all over again and "Break Forth Into Joy" hasn't been published yet. I hear the music loud and clear and have total clarity as to why I was put on this earth. In those moments, I am renewed and energized by the music of life and want to sing my song – and help others sing theirs – with confidence and joy.

And There Is Music
By Mark Cabaniss

There is music in the sound of the falling rain.
There is music in the sound of a faraway train.
There is harmony and melody in waves on the sea;
And there is music inside of me.

There is music in the sound of a mountain stream;
There is music in the sound of a favorite dream.
There is harmony and melody in all that we do
And there is music inside of you.

So let the oceans roar, and let the trumpet soar.
Celebrate the music of life.
Share your song with the world, there is so much you can say.
Where there is music, there is a way!

And let the music ring, let the singers sing.
Open up your heart to the song.
Keep your music alive, no matter what life may bring.
When you have life, there is a song to sing.

There is music in the sound of a lullaby.
There is music in the sound of a lonely wolf's cry.
There is harmony and melody in all that we do,
And there is music inside of you.

Life is beautiful for those who choose to hear the music.
And there is music, music, music.
And there is music.

Words and Music by Mark Cabaniss. Arranged by Joseph M. Martin
Copyright © 2008 by Malcolm Music and Shawnee Press, Inc.
International Copyright Secured. All Rights Reserved.
Reprinted by Permission of Hal Leonard Corporation

www.ingramcontent.com/pod-product-compliance
Lightning Source LLC
Chambersburg PA
CBHW061302110426
42742CB00012BA/2020